In the Footsteps
of
250 Years of Murder
In East London

J. P. Sperati

Edited by Louise Cissel

All correspondence for
In the Footsteps of
250 Years of Murder
In East London
should be addressed to:

Irregular Special Press
Endeavour House
170 Woodland Road
Sawston
Cambridge
CB22 3DX

*****

ISBN: 978-1-901091-80-9

Proof reading & editing: Louise Cissel
Front cover picture: The escape of John Turner by means of knotted sheets
(see *The Ratcliffe Highway Murders*).
Footprints icon: Created by Giuditta Valentina Gentile
from Noun Project
Venus de Milo icon: Created by Nuno Lezon
from the Noun Project

*****

*****

Every effort has been made to ensure accuracy, but the publishers do not hold
themselves responsible for any consequences that may arise from errors or
omissions. Whilst the contents are believed to be correct at the time of going to
press, changes may have occurred since that time or will occur during the
currency of this publication.

For JWR

CONTENTS

Introduction 7

250 Years of Murder in East London 9

1. The Hanging of a Hangman, Old Street (1718) 9
   Bunhill Fields 12

2. Dick Turpin Shoots Tom King, Aldgate East (1737) 15
   Aldgate 19

3. The Murder of Venables and Rogers, Stepney Green (1770) 21
   Stepney 23

4. The Ratcliffe Highway Murders, Shadwell/Wapping (1811) 25
   Ratcliffe 35

5. The Murder of Carlo Ferrari by 'Burkers',
   Shoreditch High Street (1831) 37
   Hoxton 44

6. Eliza Ross: The Last 'Burker', Tower Gateway/Tower Hill (1832) ... 47
   Goodman's Fields 50

7. The Case of Thomas Briggs' Hat, Hackney Wick (1864) 53
   Hackney Wick 63

8. The Artillery Passage Murder, Liverpool Street (1868) 65
   Spitalfields 69

9. The Murder of Harriet Lane, Whitechapel (1874) 71
   Whitechapel Road 77

10. The Murder of Lydia Green, Old Street (1887) 79
    Old Street 84

11. The Batty Street Murder, Aldgate East (1887) 87
    Aldgate East Underground Station 91

12. The Canonical Five Jack the Ripper Murders,
    Whitechapel/Aldgate/Aldgate East/Liverpool Street (1888) 95
    Mary Ann 'Polly' Nichols 95
    Annie Chapman 98
    Elizabeth Stride 105
    Catherine Eddowes 109
    Mary Kelly 115

13. A Double Killing in Amhurst Road, Hackney Central (1893) 123
    Hackney 127

14. The Double Murder in Turner Street, Whitechapel (1896) 129
    The Royal London Hospital 132

5

Contents

15. Murder at the Lord Nelson public house, Whitechapel (1903) 135
    Public Houses at the turn of the 20th Century 138

16. The Houndsditch Murders, Liverpool Street/Aldgate (1910) 141
    Houndsditch 148

17. The Siege of Sidney Street, Whitechapel (1911) 151
    A Policeman's Lot in 1910 158

18. The Murder of Solomon Millstein, Liverpool Street (1912) 161
    Hanbury Street 164

19. The Murder of Frances Tucker, Liverpool Street (1960) 167
    Brick Lane 169

20. The Kray Twins, Whitechapel/Bethnal Green (1966 & 1967) 171
    The Blind Beggar public house 176
    The Carpenters Arms public house 177
    W. English & Son Funeral Directors 178
    The Grave Maurice public house 178
    The Lion public house 179
    Mulberry Academy Shoreditch 180
    Pellicci's Café 180
    Repton Boxing Club & Public Baths 181
    St. James the Great Church 183
    St. Matthew's Church 184
    Vallance Road 186
    William Davis Primary School 187
    Bethnal Green 188

Maps **189**

The Krays Twins Walk **201**

Acknowledgements, References & Further Reading **213**

INTRODUCTION

To many the only crimes of note in East London are those committed by Jack the Ripper in the 19th century, and the Kray twins in the 20th century. Whereas both of these are indeed horrific, and hold a morbid fascination for some, there are many more murders to be discovered over the 250 year period covering 1718 to 1967.

The survey of murder presented here starts with Jack Ketch, a hangman, who was himself hanged for murder, and continues with the infamous highwayman, Dick Turpin, who was anything but the romantic figure often portrayed in literature. There are 2 cases of murder associated with the practice of 'Burking', and then there are the most repulsive Ratcliffe Highway murders which in many ways exceed those of Jack the Ripper for sheer brutality, especially so since one of the victims was a 14-week old baby.

Also covered is the death of Thomas Briggs who having been thrown from a moving train, became the first victim of a railway murder in the country. That case involved in an international manhunt, and resulted in the mandatory installation of communication cords on trains. Then there is what became known as the Houndsditch Murders and the Siege of Sidney Street, which began as a failed burglary of a jewellers shop by anarchists. On that night in 1910, 3 police officers were to lose their lives, making this event the largest multiple murder of police officers in peacetime Britain.

In total 20 cases are examined in this book, many of them multiple killings, and each illustrating a different aspect of murder be it the motive, means, or opportunity. Special attention is paid to the activities of the Kray twins, including a walking tour of some of the remaining locations that are most associated with them and their criminal empire.

If you find this book of interest and want to know more about East London then you may be interested in our other publications – *In the Footsteps of Jack the Ripper* & *In the Footsteps of East London Crime and Curiosities*.

East London has never seemed so bloody!

1. THE HANGING OF A HANGMAN
OLD STREET (1718)

Although not in the East End proper, Bunhill Fields does have an EC1 postcode and is only around 300 metres away from being in an E1 postcode so it seems logical to include this unusual story of murder here.

[Artist's impression of Jack Ketch from *The Autobiography of Jack Ketch* by Thomas Kibble Hervey, published in 1835 (left). Jack Ketch at work on the occasion of the execution of the 1st Duke of Monmouth on the 15th July 1685 at Tower Hill (right)]

The hangman in question was Jack Ketch (also known as John Price) who as well as being a Common Hangman, was also an ex-sailor and a habitual criminal (mainly thieving and pickpocketing). He had spent time in prison, been flogged, and even been sentenced to death for his crimes, only to have a reprieve on the recommendation of his former master who just happened to be the High Sheriff of the County of Essex.

He married, Betty, who was employed at Newgate Prison, and whom he most likely met while he was serving time there. She ran errands for the prisoners, for at that time if a prisoner could afford it, life could be made quite comfortable while inside. It was through her that he got the job of hangman for the county of Middlesex in 1713. His salary was a generous £40 per year plus the clothes of the condemned man (which he could sell). For the next 3 years he managed to stay out of trouble, though his drinking and gambling made sure that he was never far from it. Eventually his debts caught up with him, and as a consequence he spent the next 2 years at Marshalsea Prison, Southwark.

[Newgate Gaol, circa 1810 (top left), Marshalsea Prison in 1878 (top right), and Bunhill Fields in 1866 from *The Illustrated London News* (bottom)]

Ketch would have been at Marshalsea longer if he and another man had not dug a hole in the prison wall and escaped. Then around 10 p.m. on the night of 13th March 1718 as he was going through Bunhill Fields (see page 12) drunk, he came upon Elizabeth White, a watchman's wife who sold pastries and other baked goods about the streets. He attacked her savagely in an attempt to rape her. The report of the incident stated that he almost knocked one of her eyes out of her head, gave her several bruises to her body, broke one of her legs and wounded her in the belly. Two men came to her rescue and brought Ketch to the watch-house (which was built in the main to stop body snatchers – see page 37) in Old Street, where he was detained. Elizabeth was not so lucky for although she survived the evening, she died of her wounds four days later.

[The arrest of Jack Ketch]

Following Ketch's arrest, he spent 5 weeks in Newgate Prison where it was reported that he had raped a young girl who had brought food to his cell. He maintained his innocence saying that he had found Elizabeth that way, and was attempting to help her as he thought she was drunk. Appropriately enough it was back at Bunhill Fields on the 31st May 1718 that Price was hanged for murder. Shortly before his death he did make a confession but stated that he was not in control of his actions at the time due to his drinking.

BUNHILL FIELDS

[Today Bunhill Fields is popular as a quiet oasis where office workers go eat their lunch away from the hubbub of the City]

Bunhill Fields comprised 3 great fields in the Manor of Finsbury and belonged to St. Paul's Cathedral. It was semi-fen or moor stretching from the City wall to the nearest village, Hoxton. In 1498 part of the land was given over for military exercises, and in 1658 the Honourable Artillery Company moved here.

The Saxon name is thought to be a corruption of Bone Hill, indicating that it was also burial site. In 1549 around 1,000 cartloads of bones were brought here from the charnel house in St. Paul's Churchyard which literally made it a bone hill. The Corporation of London made it a new burial ground following the great plague, and built a brick wall and gates enclosing it in 1665-1666. However, there is no evidence that the site was ever actually used for plague victims, and no record of it having been consecrated. Hence, it was much used by nonconformists, and has been called 'The Cemetery of Puritan England'. It is shown on maps of the period as being Tindal's Burying Ground. After the Burials Act of 1852, Bunhill Fields was closed with the last burial in January 1854. Today the northern third of the ground is a landscaped garden and open to the public. Visitors are free to wander and discover the 2,000 or so monuments that remain from the estimated 123,000 interments that took place here.

[The graves of John Bunyan (top), Daniel Defoe (bottom left), and William Blake (bottom right) are all within a few metres of each other]

The most famous residents are John Bunyan (author of *Pilgrim's Progress*), Daniel Defoe (author of *Robinson Crusoe*), William Blake (painter, poet, and printmaker), Charles Fleetwood (son-in-law of Oliver Cromwell), Susanna Wesley (the mother of John Wesley, the founder of Methodism), and Timothy Priestly (brother of chemist Joseph Priestly credited with the discovery of oxygen).

2. Dick Turpin Shoots Tom King
Aldgate East (1737)

[Romanticised book illustrations of Dick Turpin. That on the left is of
Turpin and his horse jumping clear of Hornsey Tollgate taken from William
Ainsworth's book *Rookwood* published in 1849, while that on the right is
from a 'penny dreadful' entitled *Black Bess or the Knight of the Road*
published circa 1866]

The true story of Richard (Dick) Turpin is not the one portrayed in English folklore
where he is seen as a romantic figure akin to Robin Hood, a gentleman adventurer
and highwayman. Forget the famous overnight horse ride on Black Bess from
London to York (where he was later executed for horse theft) as that was pure
fiction from an 1834 novel called *Rookwood* written by William Harrison
Ainsworth.

Turpin started out as an apprentice butcher in Whitechapel before opening his own
shop in Thaxted, Essex. Soon after, however, in the early 1730s he joined a group
of deer thieves (providing meat for his shop) with whom he progressed from
poacher to burglar, horse thief, and finally killer. The Gregory gang as they were
known were quite brutal and on one occasion were known to have poured boiling
water over the elderly owner of a farmhouse, and also to have raped a woman there.

Public houses on the outskirts of London were common meeting places for
highwaymen to gather prior to attacking coaches making their way to the Capital.
The Spaniards on Hampstead Heath, the George at Woolwich, the Green Man on
Putney Heath, and the Old Magpie on the Bath Road would all have been familiar

to Turpin. Certainly there are newspaper reports from 1735 of Turpin carrying out robberies on the Portsmouth Road between Putney and Kingston Hill, at Blackheath and on Hackney Marshes. The last location may have been responsible for some of the romanticism associated with Turpin. The folklore says that having stopped a poor man and discovering that he only had eighteen pence, Turpin sent the man on his way half-a-crown richer.

[Turpin putting a woman on the fire while part of the Gregory gang. The incident according to the *Newgate Calendar* of 1824 took place during a robbery in Loughton]

In 1735 members of his gang were arrested but Turpin escaped. For the next two years Turpin decided to adopt a low profile until he teamed up with two new accomplices, one of whom, Tom (Robert in some references) King, he subsequently shot, probably by accident. The incident took place near the Red Lion public house at the north end of Leman Street, Aldgate on Monday 2nd May 1737. King was to die from the bullet wound to his shoulder on the 19th May, and was buried 2 days later at St. James' churchyard in Clerkenwell.

It was unfortunate for Turpin that a coachman driving into the yard of the inn recognised a bay mare that had been stolen from The Green Man in Epping the previous Saturday. He knew to whom the horse belonged and so it was not long before the rightful owner, along with constables, were keeping watch at the inn's stable to see who would come to collect the horse. Turpin and King were nearby at Goodman's Fields (see page 50), and it was King's brother, Matthew, who was sent for the mare. Matthew was followed as he left the Red Lion, and when the constables tried to make an arrest the three men resisted. In the ensuing fight Tom received the bullet wound from Turpin from which he later died.

[King as portrayed in the book *The Life and Adventures of Tom King* (left). An image from *The Complete Newgate Calendar Volume III* published in 1826 showing Turpin shooting dead Thomas Morris while hiding out in a cave in Epping Forest (right)]

Turpin fled the scene and shortly afterwards killed Thomas Morris, a servant of one of the King's keepers of Epping Forest, who attempted to capture him. He subsequently took the alias John Palmer and moved to Yorkshire where he was soon suspected of being a horse thief. He was imprisoned in York Castle for shooting a chicken in the street and for threatening to shoot its owner as well. It was again very unfortunate for Turpin that a letter he wrote while in prison to his brother-in-law back in Thaxted was handled at the local post office by the very person, James Smith, who had taught him to write at school. He recognised the writing and reported Turpin to the authorities (collecting a £200 reward for his trouble). Turpin was tried, and found guilty on two charges of horse theft. He was executed for these crimes on the 7th April 1739.

[The Old Red Lion public house, where Turpin fatally wounded Tom King, next to Aldgate East station in 1990 (left), and the same location, following a complete redevelopment of the area, in 2021 (right)]

Until recently the location of the Red Lion was easy to find as in 1903 it was rebuilt as a Watney's public house inappropriately named the Old Red Lion. However, in a major redevelopment of the area the whole block was demolished and replaced by Aldgate Tower. The site of the original Red Lion is approximately where the south entrance to Aldgate East Underground station, at the corner of Whitechapel High Street and Leman Street, is currently sited.

ALDGATE

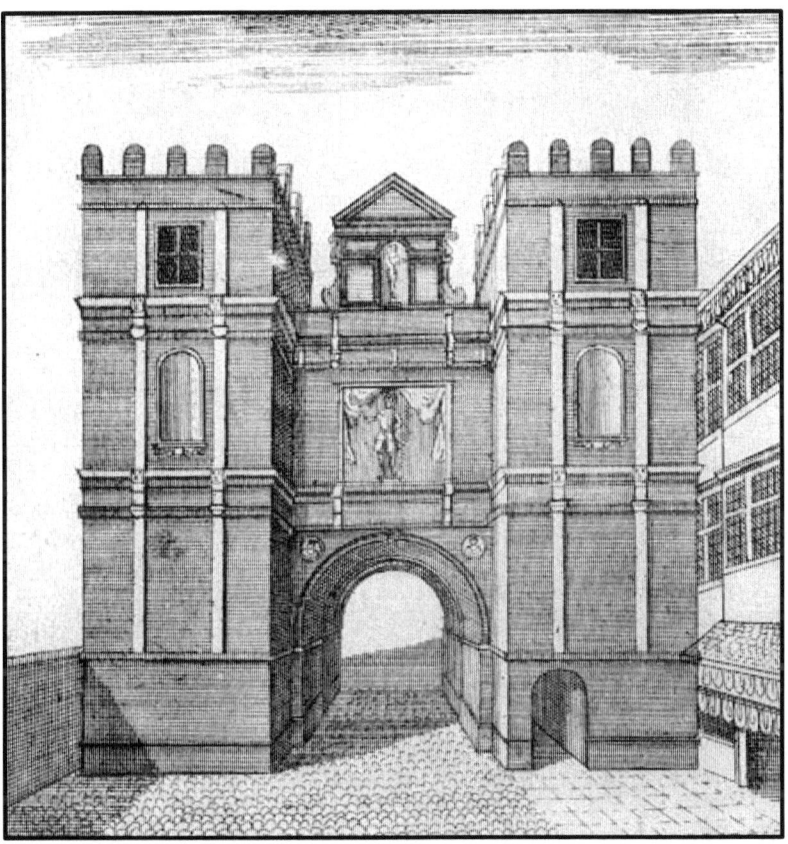

[Aldgate at the turn of the 17th century]

Aldgate was one of the 6 original City gates built by the Romans. It led out to the east toward Colchester and beyond. By Saxon times it was called Ealdgate, or old gate. It was rebuilt in the 12th century and just prior to Magna Carta in 1215 the Barons came through the gate on their way to lay siege to the Tower of London. Geoffrey Chaucer lived in a room above the gate between 1374 and 1385, and Mary Tudor entered London via the gate for the first time as queen in 1553. She was met by Princess Elizabeth along with a guard of honour comprising some 2,000 men. It was rebuilt again in 1606, and demolished in 1761.

3. The Murder of Venables and Rogers
Stepney Green (1770)

[The shooting of Venables and Rogers at Stepney Green]

As highwaymen/robbers Peter Conway and Michael Richardson were pretty incompetent for during their very first hold-up on the 27th May 1770 they shot and killed 2 men (a butcher named Venables and a carpenter named Rogers) and were so terrified by what they had done that they ran away without taking anything from their prey. The victims had been walking from Whitechapel (see page 77) to Stepney (see page 23) when the attack happened, and initially they seemed to have the upper hand since Venables twice managed to knock down both Richardson and Fox before the two assailants were in a position to fire their guns. Conway and Richardson fled to Wapping where they were more successful in robbing a man of 18s. and his watch.

[Just about the only open area today is Stepney Green Park itself, and although the exact location of the attempted robbery is not known it is through here that Venables and Rogers would have walked on their way from Whitechapel to Stepney]

There were actually 4 in the gang, the other 2 being called Jackson and Fox. Only the day before had they purchased a pair of pistols from a shop in Prince's Square near the Ratcliffe Highway (see page 35). On the day of the attempted robbery they realised that they had no ammunition, so they made bullets out of some old pewter spoons. Jackson was the first to be caught and he turned King's evidence telling the authorities who the other members of the gang were. Conway was captured next when he tried to pawn the watch, and a few days later Richardson was arrested. There is no record of Fox ever being caught. Both Conway and Richardson were tried at the Old Bailey and executed at Tyburn on the 19th July 1770, after which their bodies were removed to Bow Common where they were placed in chains on a gibbet in order to deter others who might be tempted to a life of crime. It is estimated that around 50,000 persons went to see them over the next 5 days with many people making 'money by selling liquors and other provisions to the assembled multitudes'.

STEPNEY

[St. Dunstan's Stepney/located in Stepney High Street, is one of the
most important medieval churches in London]

At the time in question the only inhabited areas in the district were those along
what is now Whitechapel Road (see page 77), Mile End Road, Stepney Green,
and beside the Thames at Ratcliffe (see page 35) – the area where the attempted
robbery took place would have been fields between Whitechapel and Stepney.

The name of Stepney is most likely from the Saxon for Stebba's landing. By
1000 the area was part of the lands belonging to the Bishop of London. It is
mentioned in the Domesday Book of 1086 as comprising of 'arable land with
some mills, good meadows, rich pastures and woodlands'. By the 16th century
Stepney consisted of 4 hamlets; Ratcliffe, Limehouse, Poplar, and Mile End (all
of which in time would become separate parishes). In 1900 the Metropolitan
Borough of Stepney was formed by amalgamating numerous parishes and
liberties to make a district with around 300,000 inhabitants. It was a poor
overcrowded area that relied heavily on the docks and the manufacture of
clothing.

23

Like most of East London it was also an area of high migration with many being Jewish, Irish, Scandinavians, and Chinese residents. World War II saw around a third of the area's buildings destroyed, which afterwards offered the opportunity for large-scale slum clearances and regeneration. Despite this, it is still considered a deprived suburb, with the only difference being that today the migrant population is mainly of Bangladeshi origin.

4. THE RATCLIFFE HIGHWAY MURDERS
SHADWELL/WAPPING (1811)

[The Marr family shop at No. 29 Ratcliffe Highway (left), and the approximate location of that premises in 2021 (right)]

At the time of the Ratcliffe Highway (see page 35) murders, in December 1811, the area was a dangerous quarter of London with seedy businesses, dark alleys and dilapidated tenements, where one in every three persons was of foreign heritage. It was at No. 29 Ratcliffe Highway (on the south side of the street located between Cannon Street Road and Artichoke Hill) that 27-year-old Timothy Marr kept a small hosier's shop (worth an estimated £180). His household comprised himself, his wife Celia (22-years-old), their 14-week old son also called Timothy, James Gowan a 13-year-old apprentice from Devon, and a servant girl named Mary (or Margaret in some references) Jewell. On Saturdays it was normal for shops to open until late in the evening. It was also pay day for staff, and therefore the day that most money would be present in the tills. On Saturday 7th December 1811 it was not until nearly midnight that the shop closed and the servant-girl was sent out to but some oysters for the family supper. This was around 2 hours later than usual.

Mary later remembered that on stepping out she saw a man standing on the opposite side of the road who appeared to be watching the shop. The shutters had been closed but not latched, and Mary left the door unlocked since she would not be long, and probably assumed that Marr would lock it behind her, though he was still busy doing paperwork in the shop. It was a fatal mistake (literally). There was

25

also a night watchman, George Olney, who was passing the building as Mary left. Unfortunately, she could find no oyster sellers open at that time of night, and returned empty-handed around 12.20 a.m. She rang the bell and also knocked on the door thinking that it must have been locked behind her. There was no answer, but she could hear sounds coming from inside, including the crying of baby Timothy. In fact, she heard somebody come to the door, and became suspicious that something was wrong when that person would not let her inside. She continued to ring the bell and ply the knocker so loudly that it alerted Olney who came to enquire if all was well. The noise also woke the next-door neighbour, a pawnbroker by the name of John Murray, who came to see what all the fuss was about.

Not being able to gain entry from the front Murray went around the back, and climbed over the 9 feet dividing wall separating the two properties. Marr's back door was wide open. He entered and went through to the shop where 'the carnage of the night stretched out on the floor, and the narrow premises so floated with gore, that it was hardly possible to escape the pollution of blood in picking out a path to the front door'. Lying by the stairs was Gowan who had his face 'smashed, his blood was dripping onto the floor, and his brains had been pulverised and cast about the walls and across the counters'.

By now a small mob were gathering outside, including a couple of watchmen. The Thames River Police, who were chiefly concerned with looting from ships in the Pool of London, were summoned. They had been founded in 1798 and predated the Metropolitan Police (which did not come into existence until 1829) and along with the Bow Street Runners were the only force at that time.

Inside all had been slain. Timothy Marr was found behind the shop counter, and his wife was nearby – both had been battered to death. Upstairs baby Timothy had been covered with pillows and blankets before having his skull crushed with a mallet and throat cut with a knife. He was still in his cot which had also been smashed to pieces. Clearly it had been a frenzied attack.

When Charles Horton, of the Thames River Police, arrived a search was made. It seemed clear that robbery was not a motive since the contents of the till were intact and in a drawer there was a further £152. The logical conclusion was that it was some sort of revenge attack on the Marr family. Upstairs a shipwright's maul covered in blood along with human hairs was found – this was evidently the murder weapon. By the back door there were two sets of bloody footprints. Some of the mob followed these and were led to Pennington Street where a witness spoke of a gang of around 10 persons who had been seen running towards New Gravel Lane (now Glamis Road) shortly after the alarm had been raised. As a result several men were arrested, including 3 sailors, but all were released due to lack of any evidence. A reward of £50 was offered.

[The funeral procession making its way to the church of St. George's in the East was watched by around 30,000 people (top left). The Hawksmoor church of St. George's in the East has changed little since it was completed in 1729 (bottom right). The 'Reward' poster (bottom left)]

At the coroner's inquest it was concluded that somebody had been watching the shop from the front for just such an opportunity to enter unobserved. Various suspects such as a carpenter (Cornelius Hart) who had been working in the shop earlier that day (who would use a maul in his work), a servant-girl who had been let go and might have a grudge against Marr, and Marr's brother with whom he had had a falling out were all questioned and then released.

Approximately 30,000 people attended the funeral of the 4 victims at the parish church of St. George's in the East the following Sunday.

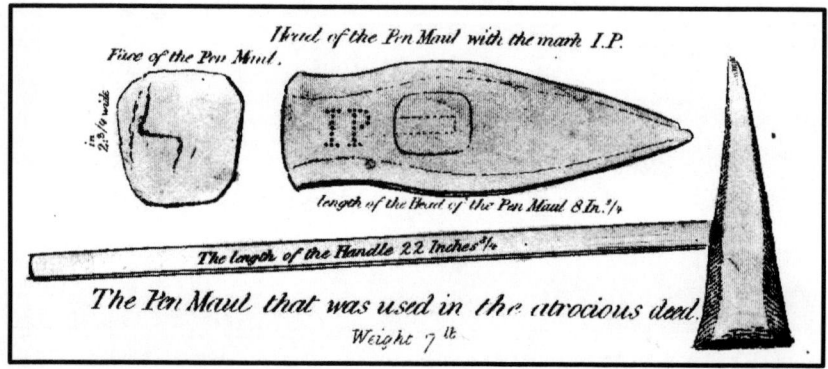

[Illustration of the maul left behind at the scene of the crime]

The sailor's maul, it was revealed, had on it the owner's initials ('IP' or possibly 'JP') carved into the handle with a copper punch, though this vital clue did not come to light until the 19th December 1811, the day of a second atrocity at the King's Arms public house in Gravel Lane (now Garnet Street) just a couple of streets away from Marr's shop. This time the landlord, John Williamson, his wife Catherine (Elizabeth in some reports), and maid-servant Bridget Harrington were all murdered, but fortunately their 14-year-old granddaughter Kitty Stilwell, asleep in her bed and unaware of what was happening downstairs, was spared. In addition, a 26-year-old lodger, John Turner, managed to escape, albeit nearly naked, from his second-floor room by tying two sheets together and using them to climb down to the street where he was met a passing watchman (see front cover illustration). The alarm was raised and soon a crowd had assembled. It is not clear how entry to the public house was achieved, for some reports say that it was via the cellar flap door in the street that was open, while others simply state that the crowd forced the front door. Either way the first body to be found was Williamson himself at the foot of the stairs to the taproom. He had been beaten with an iron crowbar, his throat cut, and his hand almost severed. In the parlour they found his wife and maid-servant, both of whom had been slaughtered in a similar manner to the Marr killings.

The crowd acted swiftly. Kitty was taken to another house for safety, fire bells were rung to call out the volunteers, and London Bridge was closed (to prevent the murderer entering South London). There were several eye witness reports of a tall man in a flushing coat (such as might be worn by a sailor) who had been loitering outside the public house earlier in the evening (and Williamson had even told one of the parish constables of such a person in a brown coat who he said had been lurking around the place and listening at the door). Turner also gave a similar description of the killer, but at that time he was a suspect himself and so his evidence was not given any credence. The Bow Street Runners were tasked with finding the killer.

[The King's Arms was demolished in the 1830s to make way for the extension to the London docks. Its location, in what is now Garnet Street, was somewhere along the dock wall (on the right of the picture) before reaching the bridge over the Shadwell Basin]

The subsequent investigation revealed that the murderer gained entry via the cellar flap, but left by an open window close to a clay-covered slope. A footprint was found in the mud and it was assumed that the killer would therefore be easy to spot as doubtless they would have both clay and bloodstains on their clothes. Local magistrates met and offered a reward of 100 guineas, with handbills being drafted within the hour. Several people were stopped but none fitted the description given. Again, it seemed that he/they had got clean away.

[The junction of Clegg Street and Cinnamon Street where Pear Tree Alley and the Pear Tree public house once stood]

There was a breakthrough, however, on the 24th December when the maul was identified as belonging to a Swedish sailor named John Petersen, but since he was away at sea when both sets of murders took place, he had a cast iron alibi. When not at sea Petersen lodged at The Pear Tree public house in Cinnamon Street, just around the corner from the Ratcliffe Highway. Indeed, it was Mr. Vermiloe, the landlord of The Pear Tree (himself in jail for debt at the time) who had come forward with this information (no doubt hoping to claim the reward and clear his debts). The police made a search of his public house and, as suspected, the maul was found to be missing from Petersen's possessions. Another lodger, Thomas de Quincey, spoke of his roommate, John Williams (a.k.a. John Murphy) who had known Timothy Marr from the time when they both worked for the East India Company and had served aboard the *Dover Castle*. Further, it transpired that there had been a grievance between the two men. This made Williams the prime suspect, as it would have been easy for him to have purloined Petersen's maul.

[John Williams]

There were several things against him being the murderer though. First, he looked nothing like the descriptions that had been given, i.e. Williams was of middle stature with vivid orange/yellow hair. Further, Turner, who claimed that he had glimpsed the murderer going about his business at the King's Arms, could not identify Williams. Finally, although Williams may have had a motive for the Marr killings, none existed for the murders at the King's Arms (especially since the Williamsons considered him a family friend), though he had been seen drinking there on the night of the killings.

From the public house Williams said that he had gone to consult a surgeon about an old wound and so had an alibi for the second event. Another factor was that Williams was in need of money and had debts, but these he was able to pay off the day after the Marr murders. Williams could explain this since he had pawned some items to raise the money, and even offered the pawn tickets up as evidence. Nobody checked either his alibi or his pawn tickets. A final piece of evidence came from Williams' laundress who said that one of his shirts appeared to have blood on the collar, but Williams explained this away saying that he had been in a brawl after a card game – it is also likely that there would be considerably more blood present on his clothing given the nature of the deed.

Williams, and 2 other unnamed suspects, were remanded in custody at Clerkenwell (Coldbath Fields Prison). He was never to have his day in court though, as on the 28th December he (apparently) used his scarf to hang himself from an iron bar in his cell. This in itself appears suspicious given that Williams had not seemed suicidal, and was in good spirits believing that he was about to be exonerated. It is quite possible that he was murdered by other inmates, or warders, or both. Most bizarrely, in the absence of the defendant, the trial still took place.

[Coldbath Fields Prison circa 1811]

31

Williams was found guilty of the murders, with his suicide being cited as clear evidence of his guilt. Williams was judged to have acted alone so all other suspects were released and the case closed.

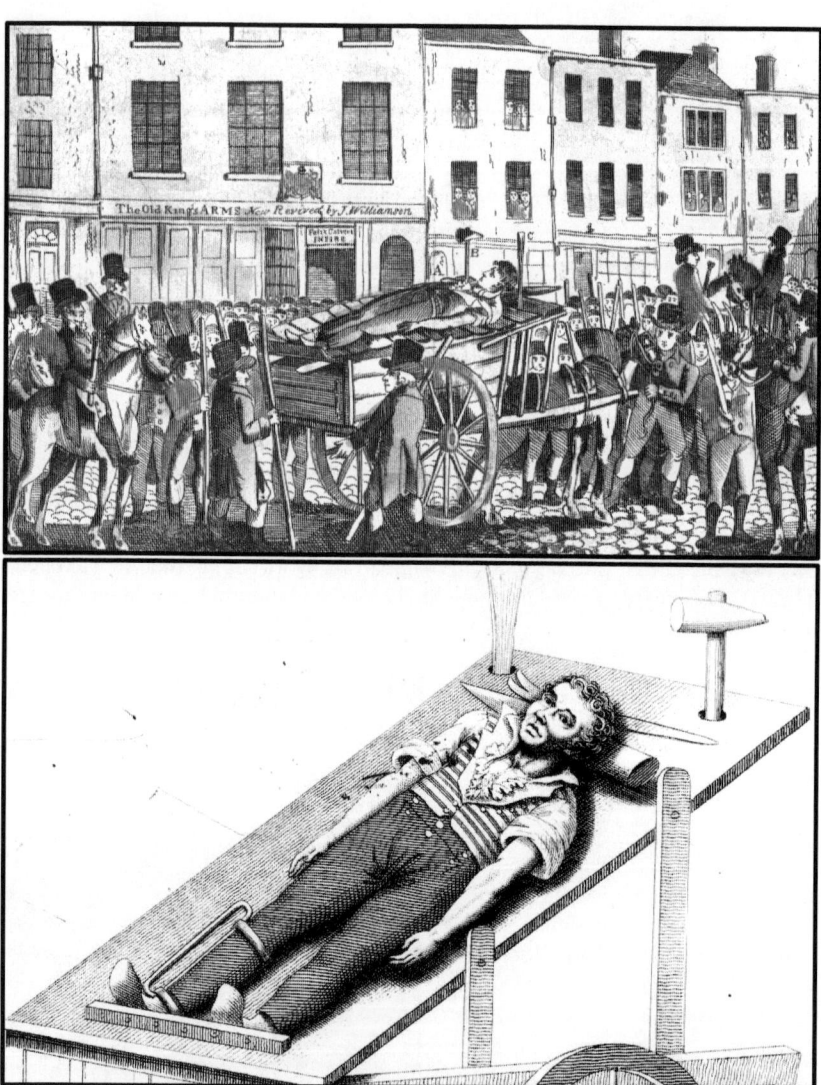

[John Williams was paraded through the streets (top). He was laid in an inclined position on a cart wearing blue trousers and a white shirt with the sleeves rolled up to expose his decaying arms (bottom)]

[The intersection of Cannon Street Road and Cable Street which became
the burial site for John Williams. Folklore has it that 100 years later when
some workmen accidentally discovered a body when installing a new mains
that the landlord of the Crown and Dolphin public house kept the skull]

The Home Secretary ordered that Williams' body be paraded through the streets
of Wapping and Shadwell so people could see the person who cheated the
hangman. The procession took place on New Year's Eve 1811 with an estimated

180,000 people turning out for the spectacle. At the point where New Road (now Commercial Road) intersects Cannon Street Road, Williams' body was tumbled out of the cart into an already dug small vertical grave (though there is more recent evidence to suggest that the location was actually at the intersection of Cable Street and Cannon Street Road). A stake was hammered through his heart. Superstition dictates that a stake through the heart keeps the restless soul from wandering. It was also believed that suicide corpses could become vampires. The significance of the crossroads was that it was supposed to confuse any evil ghost who might arise from the grave, and the grave had purposely been made too small so that even in death the incumbent would feel uncomfortable. Finally, it is likely that the body also was buried upside down so as to keep any evil spirit from escaping.

Whether Williams was the murderer or not, or acted alone will never be resolved. All that can be said for sure is that following Williams' death there were no more incidents of such horrific proportions that caused such outcry in the East End, at least not until the autumn of 1888 and the murders associated with Jack the Ripper (see page 95).

RATCLIFFE

[The Ratcliffe Highway, which in 1896 when this photograph was taken had been renamed St. George's Street]

Ratcliffe was a natural landing place on the north bank of the River Thames between the marshes of Wapping and the Isle of Dogs. The name is probably Saxon in origin being a corruption of 'red cliff' this being the colour of the soil in that part of the East End. However, there were earlier inhabitants for in 2004 a Roman bath house was excavated at the junction of The Highway (formerly the Ratcliffe Highway) and Wapping Lane.

Ratcliffe Cross was an important station for watermen, and it is said that Samuel Pepys often hired a boat from here to cross the river. A good deal of the area was taken up with wharves and warehouses, many belonging to the East India Company. Until the 19th century it was still quite rural in character, but that was to change in 1794 when the whole place was devastated by fire. It was rebuilt over the next 20 years with Commercial Road cutting through the hamlet from east to west by 1810. Other roads running in this direction are Cable Street and the Ratcliffe Highway itself.

In the late 19th century Charles Jamrach, a dealer in wild animals, opened his emporium in Ratcliffe Highway. It became the largest pet store in the world being supplied with exotic animals from the sailors visiting the Port of London. There is a story (and a commemorative plaque) about a boy who was carried off by a fully-grown Bengal tiger that had escaped from the shop. It has a happy ending though, for Jamrach gave chase and managed to prise the boy from the tiger's jaws using only his bare hands.

5. THE MURDER OF CARLO FERRARI BY 'BURKERS' SHOREDITCH HIGH STREET (1831)

The names of William Burke and William Hare who were responsible for a series of 16 killings in Edinburgh over a 10 month period in 1828 is well-known. The victims were sold on to Robert Knox for dissection at his anatomy lectures. The term 'Burker' came into the English language as somebody who provided corpses for medical use by body snatching (removal of a cadaver from a grave) or murder (usually by suffocation so as to leave no, or few, marks of violence).

The practice was widespread in the early 19th century as there was a shortage of corpses for medical research at the large teaching hospitals, especially in London. The 'going rate' for such bodies was between £7 and £9 so it could be quite profitable, and for this reason the police were extra vigilant at night around cemeteries. It also prompted some cemeteries, such as the South Metropolitan at West Norwood to construct high walls and railings to deter this practice. 'Burking' was to largely die out by the late 1830s after new laws had been enacted that ensured that there were enough bodies available for medical use.

[John Bishop, Thomas Williams, and James May]

But in 1831 'Burking' was still rife, and one notable case in London involved the trio of John Bishop (the leader), Thomas Williams, and James May. At that time Bishop was renting a property at No. 3 Nova Scotia Gardens in Bethnal Green.

37

[Nova Scotia Gardens, with a body being transported there by Bishop and Williams (left). Built on the site of a quarry where clay was extracted to produce bricks, Nova Scotia Gardens was demolished to make way for Columbia Market opened in 1869. The market failed within 5 years, but the buildings were not demolished until 1958. Only the railings from the Columbia Market Day Nursery remain. The 'Burkers' house was located just to the right of this building, which is still a nursery school today (right)]

[Bishop and Williams in the act of putting Ferrari down the well at No. 3 Nova Scotia Gardens (top). Bishop and May entering King's College carrying Ferrari's body which they hoped to sell to the School of Anatomy for dissection (bottom)]

[Carlo Ferrari (left), and Superintendent Joseph Thomas (right)]

The Bishop gang befriended a 14 year-old Italian boy called Carlo Ferrari, lured him to Nova Scotia Gardens, and gave him rum laced with laudanum. While nature took its course they adjourned to a local public house before returning and hanging the unconscious boy upside down in a well. Again they went for a drink while the boy died of drowning. They sold his teeth to a dentist, and hawked his body around various London hospitals. The School of Anatomy at King's College bought the corpse which was delivered by Bishop and May. However, soon afterwards Richard Partridge, demonstrator of anatomy, became suspicious that the body had never been buried. He called the police who arrested the 2 'resurrection' men. The police, under the direction of Superintendent Joseph Thomas, searched Nova Scotia Gardens and found Ferrari's clothes buried in the garden (along it should be noted with clothes from various other victims).

[Bishop, May, Williams, and Shields (left to right)]

40

It is not certain how many were killed at the hands of this gang – which at one time also included a fourth member, Michael Shields, a Covent Garden porter – but after his trial Bishop confessed to providing between 500 and 1,000 (mainly freshly-buried) bodies over a 12 year period.

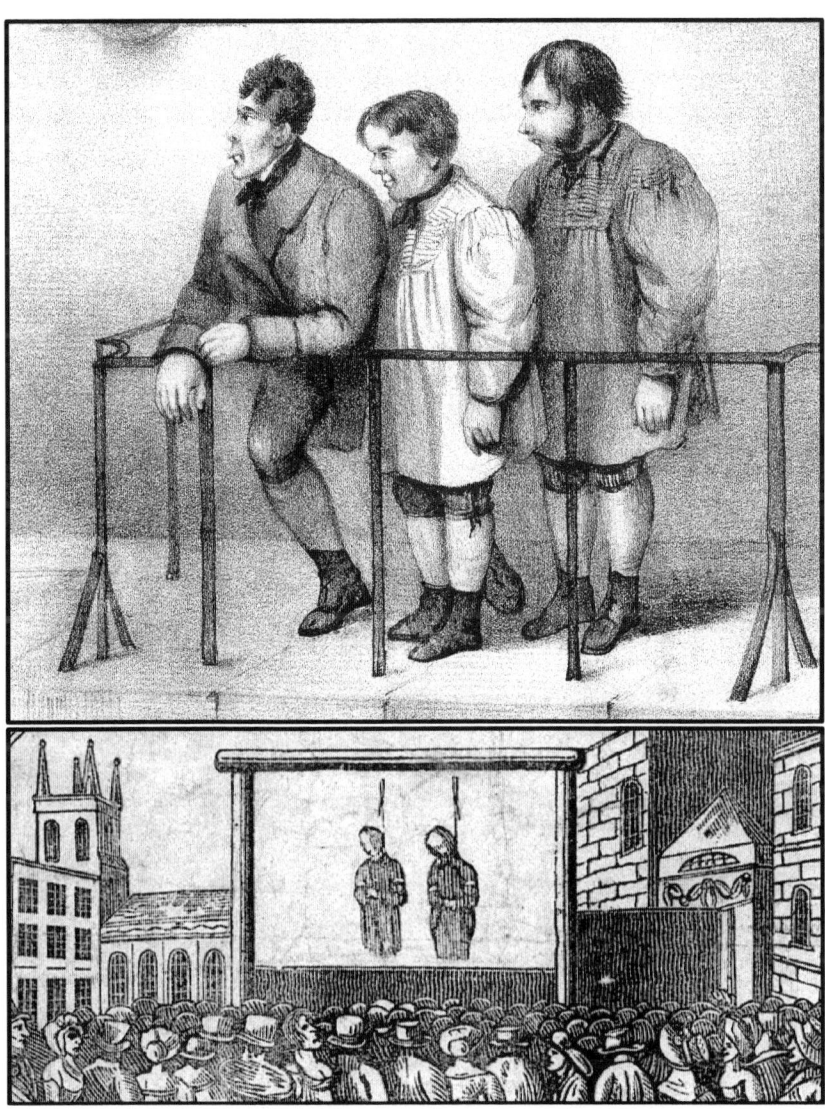

[Bishop, May, and Williams on trial at the Old Bailey (top), and the subsequent hanging of Bishop and May at Newgate (bottom)]

41

[The Theatre of Anatomy where Williams' body was sent for dissection]

Bishop and Williams were hanged at Newgate on the 5th December 1831 in front of a crowd of around 30,000. Appropriately enough their bodies were then sent for dissection (Bishop to King's College and Williams to the Theatre of Anatomy in Windmill Street) where crowds queued to see their remains. It was accepted that May had no knowledge of the murders so he was spared the gallows, and instead was transported to Van Dieman's Land (Tasmania) where he died in 1834.

Such was the interest in the case that the police opened up the cottage at Nova Scotia Gardens and charged visitors 5 shillings to see it (which included the opportunity to take away a piece of the dwelling with them as a souvenir). Although predominantly a male trade, there was at least one female 'Burker' in the East End, Eliza Ross (see page 47), who along with her husband, operated out of Goodman's Yard in Goodman's Fields (see page 50).

[View of the back garden of No. 3 Nova Scotia Gardens (top), and 'sightseers' examining the well where Ferrari was murdered (bottom)]

HOXTON

[Hoxton Hall was just one of several entertainment venues in Hoxton]

Formerly within the Borough of Hackney, Hoxton is first mentioned in the Domesday Book as a manor of 'three hides' belonging to the Canons of St. Paul's Cathedral, and remained in ecclesiastical hands until the 14th century.

In the 12th century it was described as 'fields of pasture, and open meadows, very pleasant, into which the river waters do flow, and mills are turned about with a delightful noise'. By the 16th century it was a countryside village for the wealthy and fashionable. It continued to grow and got a reputation for its market and nursery gardens.

In Tudor times there were many moated manor houses in the vicinity, including that of the Portuguese ambassador (who in his private chapel was able to celebrate Catholic mass which was illegal elsewhere in the country). To the north the fields were used for archery practice, and it was at Hoxton Fields that the playwright Ben Johnson killed actor Gabriel Spencer in a duel.

In 1605 it was to William Parker's house in Hoxton that the famous letter (probably written by Francis Tresham) warning him not to attend Parliament on the 5th November was delivered. It was responsible for foiling the Gunpowder Plot as Parker passed it on to the authorities.

During the 18th century several livery companies chose Hoxton as an ideal location for their almshouses e.g. in 1689 the sum of £20,000 was left by a member of the Haberdashers' Company for the building of almshouses for 20 freemen of the Company and also schooling for 20 sons of freemen – the result was Aske's Hospital in Pitfield Street.

In 1825 Hoxton got its own parish church dedicated to St. John the Baptist. The coming of the railways in the 1870s drove the wealthier classes away leaving Hoxton with a predominance of poor working-class people, many who lived in slums. The area became known for warehouses, factories and above all the furniture trade. By the end of the 19th century Hoxton was described as 'one of the worst parts of London, where poverty and overcrowding are characteristic of practically the whole district'.

Starting in the Victorian era Hoxton became a centre for the entertainment industry. There was the 3,000 seat Britannia Theatre (destroyed by enemy bombing during World War II), Hoxton Hall (built in 1863 as a music hall and still operational as a theatre), the Varieties Music Hall (dating from 1870 and now a cinema), Pollock's Toy Theatre shop, the National Centre for Circus Arts based in the former vestry of St. Leonard Shoreditch Electric Light Station, and most famous of all Gainsborough Film Studios located in the former power station. The studios operated between 1924 and 1951 and were responsible for a dozen Alfred Hitchcock films (though not all shot in Hoxton) including *The Lady Vanishes* (1938). Stars such as Ivor Novello, Gracie Fields, Margaret Lockwood, James Mason, Stewart Granger, Jack Warner, Petula Clark, and Patricia Roc all worked here.

[The Sir Alfred Hitchcock sculpture at the site of the former Gainsborough Film Studios]

Today Hoxton has become gentrified and has a vibrant arts scene with many bars, nightclubs, restaurants, and art galleries.

6. ELIZA ROSS: THE LAST 'BURKER'
TOWER HILL/TOWER GATEWAY (1832)

[Eliza Ross]

By the mid-1830s the trade of 'Burking' (see page 37) had died out as the Anatomy Act of 1832 provided for enough corpses to meet dissection needs for scientific research and teaching. Eliza Ross became the last person convicted of 'Burking' even though the body of her victim was never found. By all accounts Eliza was a large, muscular, fierce, alcoholic, Irishwoman who often took on male jobs such as portering. Ross was married to Edward Cook, a man 17 years her senior, and had a son also called Edward, though he was always referred to as Ned.

Eliza already had a criminal record for cudgelling cats to death and was in addition known for decoying children in order to steal their clothes. In August 1831 the three of them were resident in a garret at No. 7 Goodman's Yard adjacent to Goodman's Fields where Dick Turpin (see page 15) was nearly caught.

In December 1831 Eliza Ross and Edward Cook (now living at White Horse Court) were formally charged for the murder of 84 year-old Caroline Walsh, a street seller of sewing thread, tapes, and laces who had been lodging with them the previous August at Goodman's Yard when she went missing (only the day after moving in). The alarm was raised by Caroline's granddaughter Ann Bruton who had arranged to visit her grandmother that morning and was surprised to find her out. Repeated enquiries by her, and Caroline's other granddaughter, Lydia Basey, had yielded no trace of Caroline so eventually she had gone to the police. It was Ned who was to give the police the damning evidence against his parents. At the subsequent trial it was again Ned who became the star witness.

[No. 7 Goodman's Yard]

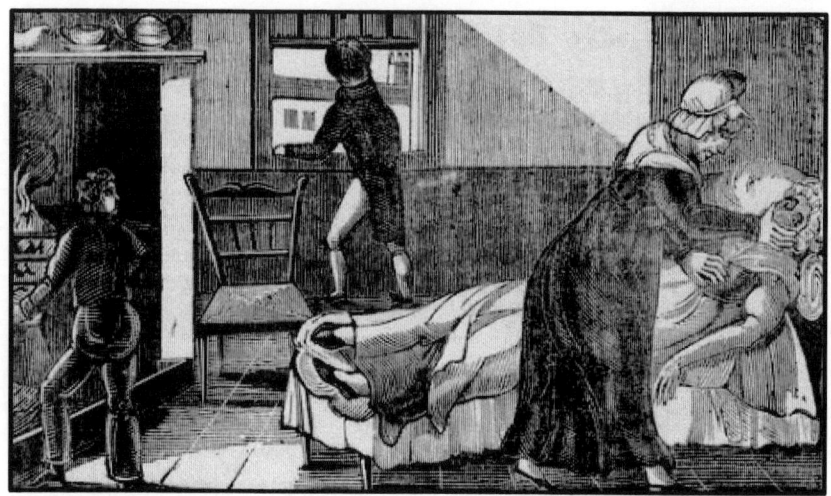

[Eliza Ross suffocating Caroline Walsh while Edward Cook looks out of the window, and Ned Cook observes all from the fireplace]

He told the court that he had watched his mother suffocate Caroline, who he implied had been drugged with a cup of coffee, before Ross placed her hand over Walsh's mouth and nose, and pressed on her chest for about 30 minutes. Edward senior had put his head out of a window so as not to observe the murder. The following morning Ned had seen a body in a sack in the cellar, and that evening saw his mother carrying the same sack thrown over her shoulders as she transported it to one of the London hospitals for sale.

[The hanging of Eliza Ross at Newgate]

Ross was found guilty (the jury taking just 15 minutes to reach their verdict) and with a large crowd in attendance was hanged at Newgate Prison on the 9th January 1832. Such was the public interest in this case (and that of Bishop, Williams, and

48

May – see page 37) that a month later the proprietor of Simmons' Waxworks in Finsbury Square offered Madame Tussaud 50 guineas if she could produce better likenesses of Bishop, Williams, and Ross.

However, there is a question mark over whether Eliza received a fair trial given that there was no physical evidence against her, and that it was mainly the testimony of Edward Cook junior that sent his mother to the gallows, though a pawnbroker in Houndsditch (see page 148) did claim that Ross had tried to sell him Caroline's clothes the day after her disappearance. Certainly Ross, rather than making a confession prior to her hanging, protested her innocence until the very end. At the trial she even went as far as blaming schoolmasters and the police for tricking or bribing her son to give false evidence. Cook junior though, never varied or retracted his statement saying, 'I said it because it was true'. Following the trial he was placed in a charitable institution, given a year of education and then went to sea (most likely having changed his name). Conversely there may have been other murders for which Ross was responsible and never charged. For example in November 1830 a 14 year-old girl, Sarah Vasey who was in service close to where Cook and Ross were then living also disappeared with there being reports soon afterwards of Eliza wearing the girl's bonnet and shoes soon afterwards.

GOODMAN'S FIELDS

[1830 map of Goodman's Fields showing Goodman's Yard where Eliza Ross murdered Caroline Walsh (top). Goodman's Yard in 2021, with the railway bridge over Mansell Street just visible to the left (bottom)]

Goodman's Fields was more of a square with trees bounded by Ayliff Street, Leman Street (so named after John Leman who developed the area, but often cited as Lemon Street by mistake), Prescot Street and Mansell Street. On Leman Street stood the Goodman's Fields Theatre (1729), the Garrick Theatre (1830), a police station (1891), the East London Industrial School (1872), a railway station (1877), and the Jew's Temporary Shelter (1886). There was also a second Goodman's Fields Theatre in Aycliff Street. Goodman's Yard was just to the west of Goodman's Fields and is a short road linking Minories and Mansell Street. In the 1640s there was a glass manufacturer here, owned by Sir Bevis Thelwell, who in 1661 provided glassware for the newly-founded Royal Society. Later it became Jesse Russell's soap and tallow factory. By 1824 there are records of an Irish Free School here, which a few years later had over 250 pupils.

[The Goodman's Fields Horses]

The railways rather destroyed the street by first building a lattice bridge to carry the (short-lived) Haydon Square extension of the London and North Eastern Railway, and then placing a good's depot there. The depot was destroyed by fire during World War II, and today the street is just another built-up, non-descript road forming part of the A1211 one-way system around Aldgate.

In the 16th century, Goodman's Fields was farmed by Roland Goodman, whose son went on to let out the fields for the grazing of horses. There is a reminder of this in 'The Goodman's Fields Horses' (6 bronze life and quarter size horses) sculpted by Hamish Mackie that can be found at Piazza Walk off Leman Street.

7. The Case of Thomas Briggs' Hat
Hackney Wick (1864)

What should have been a straight forward matter of pick pocketing escalated into an international murder hunt that became one of the most celebrated cases in Scotland Yard's history.

[The façade of Fenchurch Street station looks much the same in 2021 as it did at the time of Thomas Briggs in 1864]

The story starts at Fenchurch Street Station, the terminus of the London and Blackwall Railway, which served parts of east and north London, the docks at Tilbury, and at the other end of the line Southend-on-Sea. The station was opened in 1841 and was the first railway station in the City of London, the heart of the insurance and banking district. Thomas Briggs, a 69 year-old widower and the chief clerk at Messrs Robarts, Curtis and Co. was a regular commuter on the line between his home at No. 5 Clapton Square, where he lived with his son, and his workplace in Lombard Street.

On Saturday 9th July 1864 he dined, as usual, with a married niece in Peckham. For his return home he boarded the North London Railways' 9.50 p.m. train to

Hackney. At that time of night there were few passengers, and so the train had only three carriages, with Briggs occupying a first-class compartment in the leading one. The train was scheduled to make only 2 stops (Bow and Hackney Wick) before arriving at Hackney – a journey of just 20 minutes – after which its next working would be from Hackney to Highbury in north London.

[Hackney station, where Thomas Briggs would have alighted, with watercress beds in the foreground]

At Hackney two men, Verney and Sidney James, got into the compartment, and shortly before the departure for Highbury raised the alarm with the guard (a Mr. Ames) when they discovered that a leather cushion and seat were smeared with blood. There were clues to the previous occupant in the form of a hat (an unusual type being of black beaver with a low cut above the crown) that lay on the floor between the seats, along with a travelling bag and a walking stick with a silver knob under the seat.

Although shaken, Ames did his duty impeccably. He had the carriage locked and telegraphed Camden Town with news of a 'violent robbery, perhaps, even murder'. Only 20 minutes later a Mr. Elkin, the driver of a train of empty carriages bound for Fenchurch Street, saw a body (just a dark mound from a distance) across the tracks between Hackney Wick and Bow. He performed an emergency stop and together with the guard (a Mr. Timms) went to investigate. Briggs was miraculously still alive, albeit unconscious, so between them they carried the body (nearly being run down by a train in the other direction) to a nearby pub, the Mitford Castle, where Police Constable Edward Duggan (who had been on his beat) examined the man's clothes in an effort to ascertain his identity. Briggs still had 4 gold sovereigns and 10s 6d in silver coin on him, along with a silver snuff box. He was also still wearing and a diamond ring on his finger. However, his gold-rimmed glasses, and gold pocket watch and chain were missing (though it was easy to see where they had been torn away from his person since the gold fastening still remained attached to his waistcoat). His name was discovered from some letters found in his pocket. His son and personal physician were sent for immediately. The former was able to identify Thomas Briggs, along with his bag and the silver topped walking stick (which he had actually lent his father that day), but the hat was definitely not his (and therefore was assumed to belong to his assailant). In fact, Thomas was very particular about his dress and each year had always purchased a new hat from Messrs Dignance, a City hatters located next to the Royal Exchange.

[The Mitford Castle where Briggs was taken]

55

It seemed obvious that another passenger in his compartment had attempted to steal Briggs' pocket watch while he dosed. Briggs must have awakened, a fight ensued, and the result was that he was thrown from the moving train.

[Thomas Briggs (left), and Franz Muller (right)]

Unfortunately, Briggs died of his injuries and never regained consciousness, and thus became the victim of the very first railway murder in the country. The investigation fell to Police Inspector Tanner of K Division. He promptly had posters made up featuring the hat, and had them displayed outside every police and railway station in the Metropolitan area. There was a reward of £100 offered for any information leading to an arrest. Robarts Bank and the North London Railway matched that reward. In addition, Tanner had hatters and pawnbrokers visited.

As Charlie Chan once remarked 'When money talk, few men are deaf', and so it was to be in this instance. A jeweller in Cheapside, by the rather appropriate name of John Death (though he pronounced it Deeth), came forward 4 days later. He had been visited by a man with a German accent wishing to sell a gold chain. He had offered him £3 10s but the vendor wanted more. The jeweller would not budge in price, so instead a trade was made, in exchange for the gold chain the man took a slightly cheaper chain and a gold ring with a white stone in it. The transaction included a box with the jewellers' name inscribed upon it.

Police circulated this new information and on the 20th July a cabman named James Matthews came forward. His small daughter had been playing with a jewellers' box from Death's establishment just recently. He also recognised the description of the hat as belonging to the very person who had given his daughter the jewellers' box – a young German tailor and friend of the family called Franz Muller. In fact, it was Matthews who had purchased the hat for Muller from Messrs Walker of Marylebone. Furthermore, Matthews was able to provide a photograph and the address where Muller lodged. The information was too late though, since Muller had already left the country and was *en route* for America onboard the sailing vessel *Victoria*.

Muller's landlady, Mrs. Blyth at Old Ford Road, Victoria Park, Hackney put on record her feelings that Muller was a 'mild-mannered' man who would never commit any crime of this sort. Further his trip to America had been planned for some time and so seemed not an attempt by him to flee the country.

However, there was damning evidence to follow, in that Messrs Walker were able to confirm that the hat left on the train was one of theirs. Further from the photograph provided by Matthews, Death was able to confirm that Muller was the mystery German speaker in his shop.

Within 12 hours Tanner (accompanied by Detective Sergeant Clarke), Matthews, and Death were on their way to Liverpool to catch the steamship *City of Manchester*, which, if all went according to plan, would allow them to get to New York first. They did by two weeks, and on the morning of the 25th August 1864 a pilot boat went to meet the *Victoria*. Muller, protesting his innocence, was duly arrested. As with Dr. Crippen nearly 50 years later, Muller had been undone by taking a slow boat to New York. In his cabin Tanner found a heavy gold watch and a top hat with the initials 'DD' pencilled on the inside band.

There was an extradition hearing in New York, the result of which was far from certain given that America was in the midst of its Civil War in which Britain was perceived as interfering, but justice prevailed and Muller was returned to England to face trial.

He was defended by the German Legal Protection Society in a trial that commenced at the Old Bailey on the 27th October that year. There was much public sympathy for Muller, with hundreds having to be turned away from viewing the proceedings in the public gallery. Despite the lack of evidence, Muller had not been seen on the train, could produce alibis as to his whereabouts at the time of murder, and had people to testify as to his excellent character (including a plea from King Wilhelm I of Prussia) there were two points very much against him which taken together made a verdict of anything by guilty an impossibility.

First was that the heavy gold watch found in Muller's cabin aboard the *Victoria* was identified beyond any reasonable doubt as being the watch stolen from Briggs. Second was that the hat that Muller was wearing at the time of his arrest, although it had been altered to his style and size, could still be recognised as having once belonged to Briggs. It transpired that the initials 'DD' on the band were those of a jobbing hatter who worked for Messrs Dignance. If that were not enough, the alterations had neat stitching as would be used by a tailor, such as Muller, and not that of a hatter. Muller was found guilty and subsequently hanged at Newgate Prison on the 14th November 1864.

[The trial (top), and hanging of Franz Muller (right)]

[The exterior (top) and interior (bottom) of Briggs' train carriage would have looked similar to the images shown here]

Some good did come out of the murder though, since in 1868 it lead to communication cords being required by law on trains to ensure a method of allowing passengers to communicate with the train's guard, but only if the train was scheduled to travel more than 20 miles without stopping. It would not have helped Briggs on his short journey, but was a step in the right direction. Also the type of closed compartment with no corridor in which Briggs was travelling was soon to be phased out in favour of carriages with side corridors, and old compartment stock was modified to include a circular hole cut in the partitions which enabled occupants of neighbouring compartments to view each other and communicate. These became known as Muller's lights, but were short-lived as the communication cord superseded them as the primary safety device. It is interesting to note that as late as the 1970s trains running out of Fenchurch Street still had single compartments for 12 passengers in second-class accommodation, with only first-class having corridors (and a toilet facility).

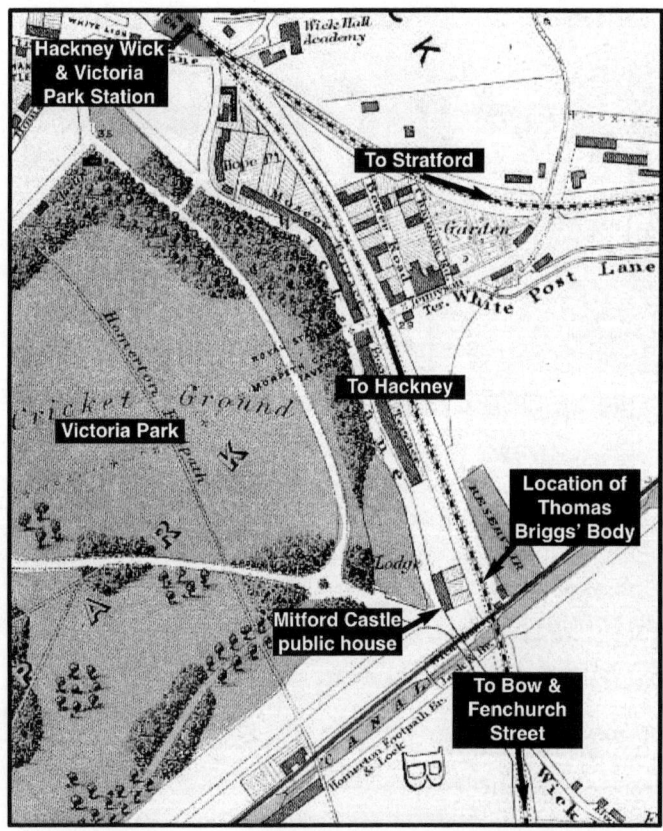

[Map of the area showing where Briggs' body was found]

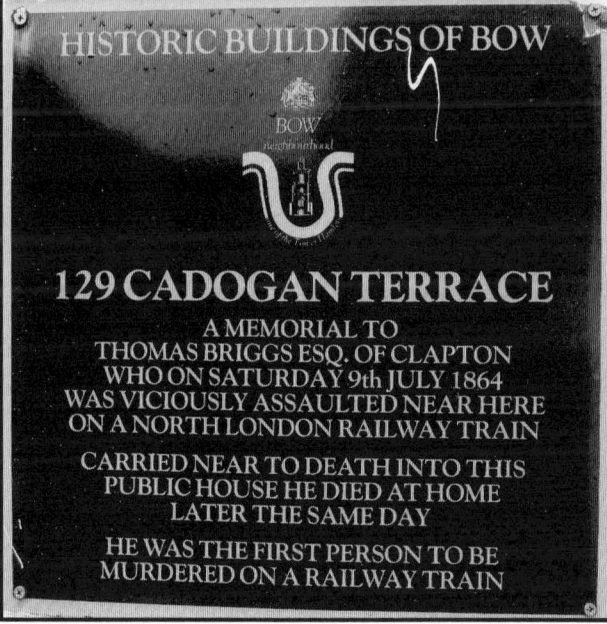

HISTORIC BUILDINGS OF BOW

BOW
neighbourhood

129 CADOGAN TERRACE

A MEMORIAL TO
THOMAS BRIGGS ESQ. OF CLAPTON
WHO ON SATURDAY 9th JULY 1864
WAS VICIOUSLY ASSAULTED NEAR HERE
ON A NORTH LONDON RAILWAY TRAIN

CARRIED NEAR TO DEATH INTO THIS
PUBLIC HOUSE HE DIED AT HOME
LATER THE SAME DAY

HE WAS THE FIRST PERSON TO BE
MURDERED ON A RAILWAY TRAIN

[The site once occupied by the Mitford Castle public house. In the background is the A12 road which is where the railway line once ran, and from where the train crew carried Thomas Briggs (top). The commemorative plaque at Cadogan Terrace (bottom)]

61

The location of the murder is known precisely since Briggs' body was found 'his foot towards London and his head towards Hackney, at a spot about two-thirds of the distance 1 mile and 414 yards between Bow and Hackney stations'. The problem is that the railway line no longer exists and is covered over by housing and the A12, but the public house to which Briggs was taken is still in existence. It is now a craft beer establishment called The Italian Job and located at No. 130 Cadogan Terrace, Hackney Wick.

HACKNEY WICK

[Typical post-industrial setting around White Post Lane with the Lee Navigation in the foreground]

In the southeast of the Borough of Hackney (see page 127) and to the west of the Lee Navigation lies Hackney Wick. In Roman times the River Lea was much wider and as a consequence in 894 a force of Danes sailed through Hackney Wick bound for Hertford. However, their venture was not successful as Alfred the Great had a new channel dug to lower the river which left the Danes stranded. The land around here was always prone to flooding, and the marshes used for the grazing of cattle. The area takes its name from a large estate, Wick Manor, upon which was Wick House. However, there was little else in the vicinity, apart from a few cottages, until the coming of the railway in the 1860s.

Following this Hackney Wick soon became industrialised, but retained a mixture of comfort and poverty – middle class living to the south of the railway line and an area of 'chronic want' to the north. This prompted Eton College to set up an urban mission here which lasted from 1880 to 1971. Industry included using the water mills along the Hackney Brook for the manufacture of silk, and from 1927 the production of shellac, a natural polymer. Other industry included the distillation of petrol, the manufacture of dyes such as Primuline (yellow) and Meldola's Blue, and the production of confectionary for Trebor Bassett (principally Clarnico Mint Creams). Another factory at White Post Lane was built for Frenchman, Eugene Serre, whose father Achille had introduced dry cleaning to England. A final claim to fame of the area was that backing onto the Lee Navigation in 1863 was the Atlas Works, which became home to the British Perforated Paper Co., where perforated toilet paper was invented in 1880.

As industry declined in the 1960s so the factories were replaced by residential properties, including 7 21-storey tower blocks on the Trowbridge estate. Conditions deteriorated quickly with much of the housing needing to be replaced by the 1980s. However, some of the former industrial sites survived and were converted to studio space, attracting a large number of professional creatives, artists, and musicians. Following the 2012 London Olympics in neighbouring Stratford the area has rapidly become gentrified.

8. The Artillery Passage Murder Liverpool Street (1868)

At No. 11 Artillery Passage was an eating house owned by George Grossmith and his wife Emma, who also had an 11-year-old son, Walter who, when not at school, helped out doing menial tasks in the kitchen – the family had been resident there since at least 1862. They employed an 18-year old live-in servant who went by the name of John, though his real name was Alexander Arthur Mackay. By all accounts Walter was an unpleasant child, while Emma was a woman of quick temper who had little patience with John who was perceived as being pretty inept at his work.

[The murder of Emma Grossmith as illustrated in
Famous Crimes Past & Present]

On the morning of the 8th May 1868 matters in the household came to a head, when Walter asked John to fetch some water so he could wash his feet. John is reported to have replied that he would be 'damned if he did' before threatening the boy by brandishing a rolling pin. Emma was on hand and scolded the servant for his action as she had done so frequently in the past. This did not improve matters of course, and Walter later related that John muttered that 'If that damned bitch does not mind, she could get into the wrong box, and get something for her trouble!'. Once Walter had gone to school, neighbours heard loud screams, and the sound of repeated blows, coming from the restaurant. This prompted their neighbour, Mary Sandiford, at No. 13, to go and knock on the door. It was answered by John, who by now had a scratch on his cheek and clothes stained with blood. Inside Emma was on the floor covered in blood, but still alive. When Mary asked if John was responsible, he coolly replied that he was not. John left, supposedly to fetch George who was just around the corner, but, not surprisingly, never returned and was seen running through the streets making his escape. A few days later he was spotted in Woolwich, near the Marine Barracks, where without any apparent care in the world, he told a friend he happened to come across that he was looking for work.

[*Illustrated Police News* image showing the murder of Emma Grossmith]

A doctor was called for Emma whose face had been so badly beaten that her husband did not recognise her. She spent several days in hospital where she recovered enough to tell George what had happened. In essence, while making pastries, John had given her a very dirty and greasy cloth for which he was again reprimanded. However, this time he had snapped and beaten Emma with the rolling pin. Unfortunately, Emma's recovery did not continue and a few days later she succumbed to her injuries. At the coroner's inquest some more information was forthcoming. First, and most importantly, John had previously spent 3 years at Feltham reformatory for larceny. In addition, his work at the eating house had involved long hours and low pay, and he was known to have a temper. The verdict was one of wilful murder, but that was of little consequence without an arrest.

[Artillery Passage in 2021. No. 11 where Alexander Mackay murdered Emma Grossmith is the restaurant on the left-hand-side of the image]

In July the police had the notion that John might already be in prison only under a false name. Luckily when he fled No. 11 Artillery Passage, he left behind in his bedroom a photograph of himself. The police had it copied and circulated it to various provincial police forces and prisons. The image matched that of George Jackson who was serving time for theft at Maidstone Prison. John was promptly brought back to London and put on trial at the Old Bailey. He was found guilty on the 17th August, and executed at Newgate Prison on the 8th September 1868. The Grossmith family continued their eating house business until 1881. The premises is still a restaurant.

SPITALFIELDS

[Spitalfields today with the 18th century Christ Church still dominating the area. The large building to the right is the London Fruit and Wool Exchange, while to the left is the roof of Spitalfields Market itself]

The fields in question were those to the east of the medieval priory and hospital of St. Mary Spital, where a Roman cemetery was discovered in the 16th century. According to Daniel Defoe 'the lanes were deep, dirty and unfrequented, the part now called Spitalfields Market was a field of grass with cows feeding on it. Brick Lane, which is now a long well paved street, was a dirty road, frequented chiefly by carts fetching bricks that way into Whitechapel from brick kilns in those fields'.

In 1537 part of the fields were given over as an artillery ground where members of the Guild of Artillery could practice with their longbows, crossbows, and guns. In 1682 the old artillery ground was purchased by four wealthy property speculators, and as early as 1640 buildings started to appear at the Whitechapel end of the fields, so that by 1675 there were around 1,300 houses there. These were small tenements crowded into narrow streets and alleyways. Today the street layout remains virtually unchanged from that of the late 17th with Artillery Lane being a main thoroughfare leading east from Bishopsgate (the A10) to its junction with Crispin Street and Bell Lane. A reminder of its former use comes from Gun Street and Fort Street which lead off from Artillery Lane.

Artillery Passage is one of those narrow alleyways running between Artillery Lane and Sandys Row.

9. THE MURDER OF HARRIET LANE WHITECHAPEL (1874)

[Wainwright's warehouse in Whitechapel Road (left) and Wainwright on one of his frequent visits to the theatre (right)]

Henry Wainwright was not a man who did things by halves. He was a respectable businessman who had two brush-making concerns (a factory and a warehouse) in the Whitechapel Road (at Nos. 84 and 215 – almost opposite each other and close to Whitechapel Underground Station and the London Hospital). He had a wife and 4 children who lived at No. 40 Tredegar Square, and a brother, Thomas, who kept an ironmonger's shop operating out of a disused public house called the Hen and Chickens located the other side of the River Thames in Borough High Street. Henry also kept two mistresses and had a passion for seducing women from theatrical backgrounds (whom he often first met at the Pavilion Theatre which was adjacent to his factory). He was also a temperance lecturer.

His first mistress was Harriet Lane, an apprentice milliner, whom he met in 1871 when she was just 20 years-old. He set her up in a lodging in the West End under the name of Mrs. Percy King, and gave her a generous allowance of £5 a week. Harriet was to have two children, almost certainly by Henry. His second mistress was a young ballet dancer named Alice Day whom he also kept in a similar manner.

It may have been the distraction of 3 women and multiple children, or just that he wasn't as good a businessman as his late father, that caused his financial position to decline to the point of bankruptcy. Cut backs had to be made starting with the family home and a move to a more modest residence in Chingford. He also decided to dispose of one of his mistresses, and the obvious choice in this respect

71

was Harriet who had become something of a liability through her frequent nagging and angry scenes when drunk. So, on the 10th September 1874 Henry invited her to the factory at No. 215 Whitechapel Road. When she arrived the following afternoon, having told her family that she was meeting a Mr. Frieake, she was first shot in the head and then had her throat cut prior to being buried under the floorboards at the rear of the paint workshop.

[Harriet Lane (left), and Wainwright in the act of murder (right)]

Luckily for Henry she had few friends and was not missed. Any enquirers were told that she had gone away to travel and live in Europe with a new man friend. In fact, the story was substantiated by the fact that at some earlier point, when Henry was already growing tired of Harriet and her threats to expose their affair, he had persuaded brother Thomas (using the pseudonym Edward Frieake) to court her in the hope of taking the pressure off of Henry (or perhaps to lay the groundwork for her disappearance). Henry was even able to show Mrs. Wilmore, a close friend of Harriet's who looked after the children when she was away, a letter from Frieake stating that he and Harriet were going to be married and that afterwards they were both determined to begin a new life together cutting off all communication with friends and family. Some months later there was a telegram, again supposedly from Frieake, stating that the couple were just off to Paris 'to have a jolly spree'. To calm matters down Henry began making (irregular) payments to Mrs. Wilmore for the children's care. As time passed it looked like Henry would get away with murder, since the body had not been discovered.

The financial situation did not improve however, and in November of the same year his factory at No. 84 Whitechapel Road burnt down. The insurers wisely refused not to pay since they suspected arson. In June the following year Henry finally went bankrupt and a solicitor called Behrend was engaged to salvage what he could from the business. Consequently tenants moved into No. 215 Whitechapel Road, but soon moved out again due to a foul smell, which they thought was coming from the rear of the building. The property was put up for sale, and this prompted some action on the part of Henry lest any new owners were to find the body.

So exactly one year after Harriet's invitation to visit his factory, Henry used his set of keys to enter the empty building and retrieve what remained of Harriet. The body was remarkably well preserved due to the fact that Henry had used chloride of lime (a disinfectant and preservative) instead of quicklime (which accelerates the decay process) when burying Harriet originally. He chopped the body up into small parts, packed them into two large canvas parcels, and went home for the night.

[**Wainwright recovering the body of Harriet Lane in his empty factory a year after murdering her (left). Alfred Stokes (right)**]

The next day he asked a former workman of his, Alfred Stokes, to help in moving the parcels to his brother's shop in Borough – in fact, the business had recently failed and the building was empty, though Thomas still held the property lease. Possibly unknown to Thomas, Henry had a set of keys to the shop. Stokes agreed but as they walked from Whitechapel he soon complained of the smell emanating from the parcels. Thinking on his feet, Henry went off to get a taxi from the nearest cab rank during which time Stokes decided to look inside one of the parcels. When Henry arrived back with a four-wheeled cab (No. 8505) he thanked Stokes for his help and went off alone in the vehicle. By now the game was almost up, for Stokes

73

knew that some sort of crime had been committed and tried following the cab on foot. In Leadenhall Street, close to the Hop Exchange, he came across two policemen and asked them to stop the cab. They refused thinking Stokes a madman.

[The arrest of Wainwright by Police Constable Turner]

Just as it looked like Henry would get away, he came across Alice Day walking along the street. For what could only be regarded as an act of extreme stupidity, he had the cab stop and offer her a ride. She accepted, and to disguise the smell of the rotting limbs, Henry lit up a large cigar. The stop gave Stokes time to catch up with the vehicle, and he was able to follow it all the way to its destination at

No. 54 Borough High Street. Henry entered the Hen and Chickens with the first parcel, leaving Alice in the vehicle guarding the second. Meanwhile Stokes happened across Police Constable Henry Turner on patrol and implored him to investigate the suspicious packages. Soon another constable was also at the scene, and despite an offer by Wainwright of first £50, and then £200, for them to walk away, they did their duty. The arrest of Henry and Alice was made on the spot, and that of Thomas followed later when he could be found.

[Thomas (left) and Henry Wainwright (right) in the dock (left). Vine Court in 2021. The building with the chimney behind is all that remains of Wainwright's warehouse that fronted No. 215 Whitechapel Road (right)]

Alice was soon released since there was nothing to incriminate her, but Thomas was sentenced to 7 years as an accessory after the fact, while Henry was found guilty of murder and hanged at Newgate Prison on the 21st December 1875. It might well be that Thomas got off lightly, even though he may not have known anything about the murder itself. It is possible that Henry was going to put Harriet in the cellar without Thomas' knowledge. The question has to be asked, if Thomas was a true accomplish why then did Henry not ask him to help move the parcels, rather than reply on a former employee? Given that Thomas had already been persuaded to play the role of suitor to Harriet, if subsequently her remains were found in his cellar, the most logical suspect for murder would be Thomas himself (in the absence of a confession from brother Henry). It is quite likely, therefore, that Thomas was guilty only of being gullible and trying to help his brother, who in return had a long-term plan to frame him for murder if matters came to ahead.

Although both the Wainwright factories are long gone, the paint shop where Harriet was murdered does still exist and is located in Vine Court close to the junction with Whitechapel Road (No. 130 which today corresponds to No. 215 in 1874).

WHITECHAPEL ROAD

[A congested Whitechapel High Street looking toward Whitechapel Road and St. Mary's church, circa 1905]

Whitechapel Road takes its name from the 14th century white chapel which stood at the east end of the road. The Whitechapel Bell Foundry and the Royal London Hospital (see page 132) are both located here.

The bell foundry was established in 1420 in Houndsditch, but moved to Whitechapel Road in 1738, taking over the grounds and buildings of the Artichoke Inn. Many of the world's great bells have been cast here, including those for Westminster Abbey, Big Ben, and America's original Liberty Bell.

In 1695 the body of Trinity House set up Trinity Green almshouses for retired seamen just to the east of where Whitechapel Underground station is located today. The 2 rows of houses with a central green and chapel remain the oldest almshouses in London.

The first major theatre, The Pavilion Theatre, to open in the East End did so in 1828 on the site of a former clothes factory at Nos. 191-193 Whitechapel Road. It stayed in business until 1934. Whitechapel Road was also the eastern terminus of the MailRail, the Post Office automated underground railway which ran between 1927 and 2003. Another long-term business in the road was the Albion Brewery which was established in 1808 by Richard Ivory, who was the landlord of the Blind Beggar public house (see page 176). At its peak it produced 133,000 barrels of beer a year, but closed in 1979.

From 1884 a famous resident was Joseph Merrick, better known as 'The Elephant Man', who was 'put on display' in the back room of a shop opposite the London Hospital. Later he was to make his home in a room in the hospital, where he spent the last years of his tragic life.

Finally, it was in Whitechapel Road, close to the Vine Tavern, that Methodist William Booth preached the doctrine which led to the foundation of the Salvation Army. He is commemorated by 2 memorials (and another to his wife Catherine) close to Trinity Green.

10. The Murder of Lydia Green Old Street (1887)

It is against a backdrop of poverty and overcrowding that in around 1870 Ann Green leased a large terraced house at No. 8 Baches Street. She lived in the basement kitchen with her 3 young daughters and let out all the other rooms. In total the residence was home to 18 persons. Ann's eldest daughter, Alice, married William Thomas Gauntlett in 1884, but he died just two years later forcing Alice to return to Baches Street along with her new born son. The middle daughter, Lydia, was to have a long-term relationship with Thomas William Currell, a soldier in the Middlesex Fusiliers. They became engaged when she was 19-years old, and were still engaged in 1886, having by then known each other for 10 years.

Currell left the army with the rank of corporal, but being without a trade or education he could only find civilian work as a sponge-trimmer. He was a heavy drinker and over time became a loafer. He fell into financial difficulties and by 1887 he was penniless, a drunk, and out of work.

On Saturday 5th February 1887 Alice went out early in the morning leaving Lydia with her baby. A little later Caroline Sinclair, a lodger on the second floor, and John Thomas, a lodger on the third floor, were both awakened by a loud noise. Ann Green heard 3 loud bangs as if something heavy had fallen down. Upon investigation Lydia was found dead in her bedroom with blood on her head and face, but Alice's baby was alive and well. Dr. Davis at first thought that death had been the result of a fall in which Lydia's neck had been broken. He was to revise his opinion on consideration of the bleeding from injuries to the right hand and to the side of the throat to be death from a stabbing. The post-mortem revealed that Lydia had actually been shot with a small-calibre revolver, one bullet being lodged in her brain and another in her jaw.

Another lodger, Thomas Attrell, came forward with information that he had met Currell at 7.30 a.m. and had had a drink with him at the Crosby Head public house. This in itself had seemed suspicious, but even more so when he revealed that Currell had asked him for his latch key on the pretext that he wanted to remove some items from the kitchen without disturbing the family.

Police searched Currell's lodgings and found a box of cartridges which were a match for those that had killed Lydia. 'Wanted' posters with a daguerreotype (an early photographic process invented by Louis-Jacques-Mandé Gaguerre in 1839) portrait of Currell were posted all over the Metropolis. Given that Currell was a known drunk and penniless the police expected to wrap this case up quickly.

However, this was not to be for Currell gave them a good 'run for their money' for 10 days.

[*The Penny Illustrated Paper* gave front page coverage to what they called the 'Hoxton Murder', though today it would be considered to be Old Street]

[The arrest of Currell was featured in a double page spread in *The Penny Illustrated Paper* (19th February 1887) just a week after they had broken the news about the 'Hoxton Murder']

Currell had first gone to Lydia's workplace, before her demise was known, and cashed in her unpaid earnings. The police managed to trace him to a lodging-house in Hampstead, but he had already gone from there by the time they interviewed his landlady, Mrs Smith. There was then a strange turn of events when on the 15th February Detective Inspector Peel of G Division received a letter from Currell stating that he wished to give himself up the following day at St. Mary's Church in Islington. He did not turn up, but shortly afterwards he was spotted nearby, a chase ensued and he was arrested. The reason why Currell had not been captured earlier became all too apparent – since the murder he had sobered up, shaved, and bought new clothes with the money he had purloined from Lydia's workplace, and he no longer resembled the daguerreotype image on the 'wanted' posters. If he had not written to Peel he could easily have gotten away and started a new life.

Currell was duly tried at the Old Bailey, and was found guilty. He was executed at Newgate Prison on the 18th April 1887. After the verdict he made a full confession saying that he acted on a sudden impulse to shoot Lydia after some heavy drinking. The revolver, which he had only purchased a few days before, he had thrown into the Regent's Canal.

[The final mention of Currell in *The Penny Illustrated Paper* was on the 23rd April 1887 as he awaited his execution]

**[Nothing remains of Victorian Baches Street. No. 8, where
Lydia Green was murdered, is still a residential block]**

The 1894 Ordnance Survey map shows Baches Street as being made up of houses along the majority of both sides of the street, but with a 'glass manufactory' on the southeast corner. The dwellings were described as 'mixed, some comfortable, others poor'. By 1898 the street had changed with 'only a few dwelling houses at the northeast and southeast end left ... the rest having been replaced by large factories'. No. 8 Baches Street, where the murder of Lydia Green took place, was on the east side of the street, and soon to be adjacent to the 'glass manufactory' which by 1894 took up the even Nos. 2-6.

OLD STREET

[St. Leonard's, Shoreditch has a dominant position at the junction of Old Street, Hackney Road, Kingsland Road, and Shoreditch High Street]

Simply named 'for that it was the old highway from Aldersgate for the north-east parts of England, before Bishopsgate was built', today Old Street extends from Goswell Road (Clerkenwell) to Shoreditch. It was first recorded in around 1200 as Ealdestrate, and later it became Oldestrete, though it is possible that there was some form of road here in pre-Roman times. If this is so, then Old Street would have skirted around the walls of what is now the City of London. In fact, today the eastern half of the road forms part of the London Inner Ring Road. The other end of the road was widened between 1872 and 1877, with only a few domestic buildings dating from the 18th and early 19th centuries still standing.

At its eastern end, Old Street joins the old Roman road to York at what can be considered the civic hub of Shoreditch, for this is where Shoreditch Town Hall, Shoreditch Magistrates Court, and the church of St. Leonard's, Shoreditch can be found. The current church, built in the Palladian style by George Dance the Elder, dates from 1740, though there is evidence of a former Saxon building on the same site.

['Silicon Roundabout' with large electronic advertising hoarding]

Although for most of its length Old Street consists of nondescript buildings, more recently, in the vicinity of Old Street roundabout, a number of IT and technology companies have set up offices such that the area has now become known as 'Silicon Roundabout'. This is also where between 1766 and 1864 the City turnpike stood, and is the present location Old Street Underground station.

11. THE BATTY STREET MURDER ALDGATE EAST (1887)

The Israel Lipski case, on the face of it, is very much an open-and-shut one, but it presents some interesting points and even has a Jack the Ripper (see page 95) connection. It was in 1886 that Israel Lipski, whose real surname was Lobulsk, and Miriam Angel both arrived in England from their native Poland. He set up an umbrella and walking-stick business in which he employed 2 workmen named Harry Schmuss and Henry Rosenbloom. Lipski and Angel were living in the same boarding house at No. 16 Batty Street, Whitechapel (where coincidentally the landlady's surname was Lipski also).

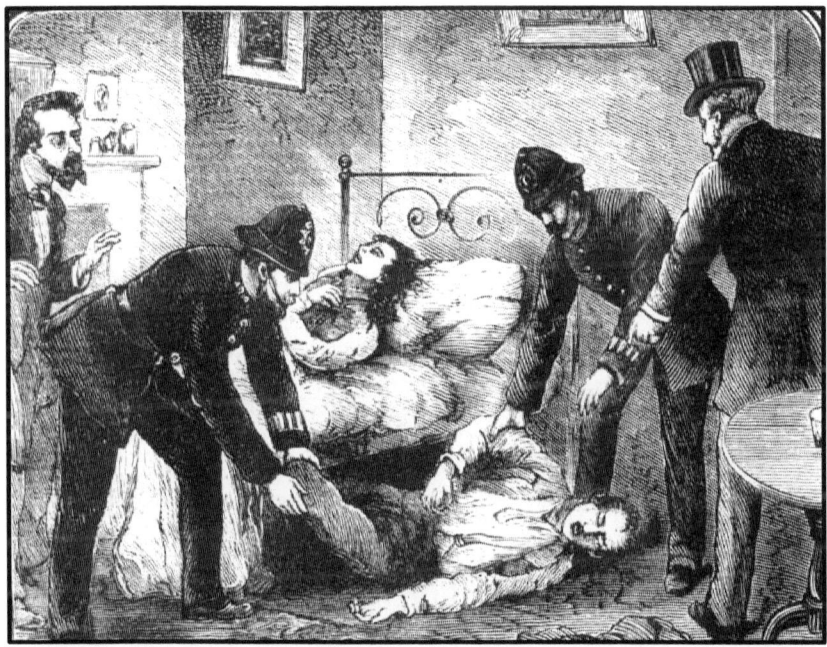

[Image from *The Illustrated Police News* showing Lipski being removed from under the bed in Miriam Angel's room]

On the morning of the 28th June 1887 Miriam was found dead in her 1st floor bedroom – she had been forced to consume *aquafortis* (nitric acid). What is more she was 6 months pregnant. The 22-year old Lipski, who lodged on an upper floor, was found hiding under her bed and exhibited acid burns in and around his mouth. It seemed clear that he was responsible, but there was no evident motive, and furthermore there was no reason why he would want to take nitric acid himself,

87

unless it was in remorse for what he had just done. The door to the room had also been locked from the inside indicating that no other persons had been present.

For his part Lipski insisted that he was innocent and that he happened upon Schmuss and Rosenbloom in Miriam's room. They were in the act of burglary, having already killed Miriam with the acid. On seeing Lipski they turned their attention on him, poured the nitric acid down his throat before throwing him under the bed where he passed out. The police were convinced otherwise and that it was a simple matter of attempted rape that had gone wrong.

Lipski was himself engaged to a Jewish girl named Kate Lance so it might seem unlikely that he would be drawn to rape. It also came to light that Schmuss was a qualified locksmith and so would have no trouble in making it look like the door had been locked from the inside. However, damning evidence against Lipski was soon forthcoming when it was revealed that earlier that day Lipski had purchased an ounce of nitric acid.

[More coverage of the case was given in the 27th August 1887 issue of *The Penny Illustrated Paper*]

At trial Lipski was found guilty and sentenced to death. Lipski's legal defence was abysmal and by today's standards the judge, James Stephen, would be considered biased and anti-Semitic. Even at that time there were several prominent people who feared that the trial had been unfair and called upon the Home Secretary, Henry Matthews, for a reprieve or commutation. It had no affect and Lipski was hanged at Newgate Prison on the 21st August 1887, but not before he made a written confession.

In that document he stated that his intention was always robbery and not to violate Miriam. The nitric acid that he had purchased that morning he claimed for his own suicide as he 'had long been tired of my life'. When Miriam awoke he remembered the acid bottle in his pocket and used it to quieten her, rather than kill. Realising what he had done he then drank the rest himself, and upon hearing the footsteps upon the stairs hid under the bed. Those of a more charitable disposition toward Lipski claim that he only made this confession so he would not be thought of as a rapist. Others say that he intended murder all the time on account of Miriam having told him that her unborn child was his – this would not have gone down well with his fiancée.

Whichever version is the truth Lipski was guilty of murder and received the penalty for that crime, albeit via a questionable trial. It must be remembered that at that time there was a climate of pervasive anti-Semitism in East London with the Jewish population of mainly poor Polish and Russian refugees being blamed for most of the social problems of the area. In fact, even before his execution the word Lipski was to become a verb (e.g. I am going to 'Lipski' that woman) as well as a general slur against Jewish people.

[Lipski on trial at the Old Bailey (left), and Israel Schwartz observing Elizabeth Stride talking with an unidentified man (most likely Jack the Ripper) who shouted back 'Lipski' at him (right)]

During the Jack the Ripper investigation it was reported by Israel Schwartz that he saw a woman, later identified as Elizabeth Stride (see page 105), being assaulted in Berner Street with the attacker shouting out the word 'Lipski'. Police had to judge whether this was the surname of Jack the Ripper, or was being used as an ethnic slur against Jews in general. There were several Lipskis living in the immediate area, but upon investigation the police decided on the latter explanation.

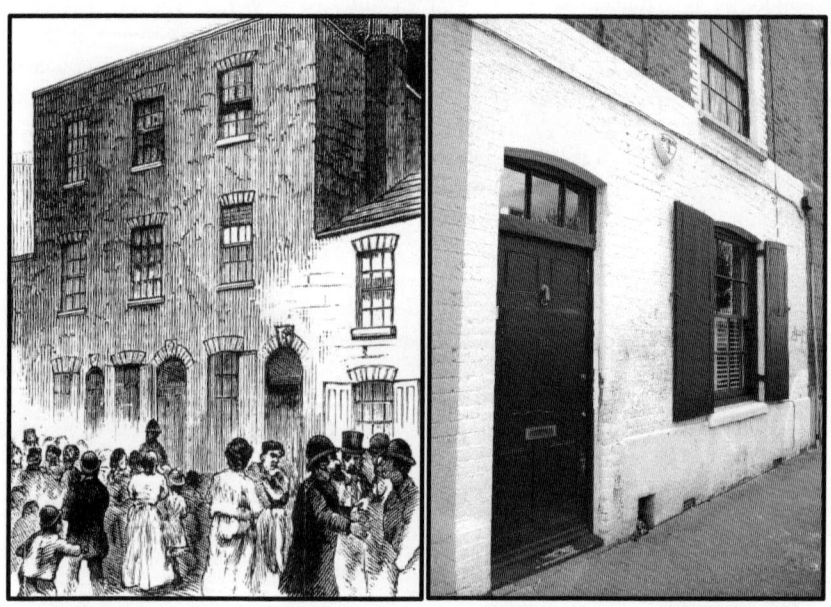

[Crowds gather outside No. 16 Batty Street after the murder (left). The façade of No. 16 Batty Street looks little changed since 1887, although neighbouring buildings are more modern and an extra storey seems to have been added (either that or *The Illustrated Police News* artist made a mistake which is unlikely) (right)]

ALDGATE EAST

[The entrance to the original Aldgate East Underground station that
was around 150 metres to the west of the current station]

When the London Underground was opened in 1863 it was not the consolidated
single system that it is today. It was comprised of a group of privately owned
and managed routes that were not necessarily connected or coordinated. Aldgate
East station, which was originally going to be called Commercial Road, was
opened on the 6th October 1884 as an extension to the District Railway. Later,
when the Metropolitan Railway reached Aldgate from Liverpool Street it
necessitated a particularly sharp curve in order to avoid Aldgate East station – in
fact, a triangular junction was formed with Aldgate East, Liverpool Street and
Mark Lane stations at the vertices.

It was never a very satisfactory arrangement for the running of trains so the
London Passenger Transport Board under the 1935-1940 New Works
Programme proposed enlarging the triangular junction to produce a much gentler
curve, and to ensure that any trains held on the curves would not interfere with
the various sets of points or signals. As a direct consequence, Aldgate East
station had to be moved 150 metres further east, meaning that it would now be
that much closer to St. Mary's (Whitechapel Road) station which it was decided

91

could be closed. This made sense since stations in this part of London would now be more evenly spaced, and money (as well as travel time) could be saved with the closure of St. Mary's (Whitechapel) station.

[**The suspended tracks, on which trains continued to run, are almost ready to be lowered into position alongside the new platforms (top), and the station in 2021 which has more headroom than most (bottom)**]

The new Aldgate East station needed to be on a straight and level section of track, before a fairly sharp incline up to Whitechapel station. The maths showed that the new track bed needed to be just over 2 metres lower than the existing one. The problem was how to excavate this whilst still keeping trains running. The answer was simple in that the existing track was held up by a timber trestle framework attached to hooks in the roof while work carried on below. Passengers were often surprised when passing through the construction site to see the new station below – it was as if their train had become an aeroplane which had just taken off!

[The hooks that held the track are still in place today]

When work was complete over 900 workmen in a single night lowered the tracks into position so that the new station could open on the 31st October 1938. If you visit Aldgate East station today you can still see the hooks in the roof that held up the track, and will also notice how much higher the roof is at this station over others on the network. In addition, if you travel from here to Liverpool Street station you can also see on the right-hand side (especially if the train is held on the section of track between Aldgate East and the Aldgate curve as is frequent) the old Aldgate East platforms and pedestrian bridge frozen in time.

12. THE CANONICAL FIVE JACK THE RIPPER MURDERS WHITECHAPEL/ALDGATE EAST/LIVERPOOL STREET (1888)

There is no particular agreement among historians, the police, or the 'Ripperlogists' as to just how many murders can be attributed to Jack the Ripper since one of the many dangers of being a female prostitute in the East End at that time was violent death. However, it is generally agreed that there were at least 5 victims, these being known as the canonical 5, and it is these that will be considered here. For a more detailed account of Jack the Ripper, including a new solution to the case and a look at other possible victims, please see our sister publication *In The Footsteps Of Jack The Ripper* from which the extracts below are taken.

MARY ANN 'POLLY' NICHOLS, WHITECHAPEL

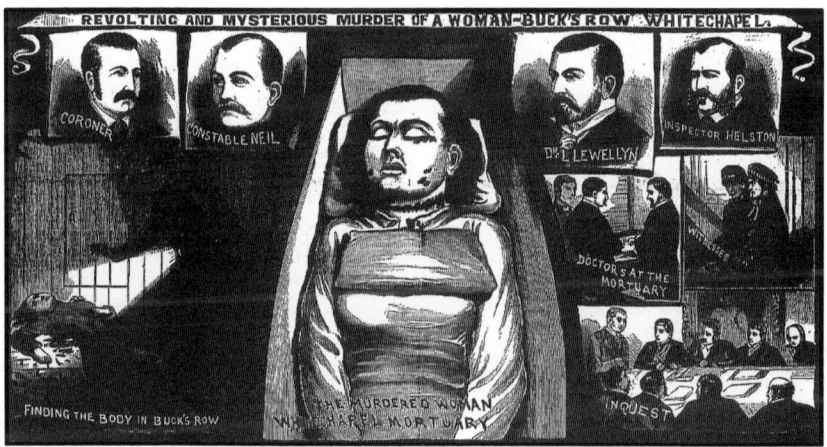

[*The Illustrated Police News* drawings of the Mary Nichols murder]

For Police Constable John Neil it started as a night on the beat like any other, but at around 3.45 a.m. he came across the body of a woman lying on the pavement close to a stable-yard in connection with Essex Wharf in Buck's Row (now Durward Street) which runs parallel with the railway line close to Whitechapel Underground station opened in 1876. At first, and because the street had only a single light at the eastern end, he assumed that the woman had fallen down drunk and was merely sleeping off the effects of her drinking. However, closer inspection revealed that her face was stained with blood and that her throat had been cut from ear-to-ear.

[Buck's Row in Victorian times (top left), the gated stable entrance
where Police Constable Neil found the body of Mary Nichols (top right),
as reported in the press (bottom left), and the same spot in 2021 – the stable
entrance being by the Durward Street exit to Whitechapel station with the
former Buck's Row Board School, now Trinity Hall
residential flats, in the background (bottom right)]

In fact, Neil was not the first to see the body, for only a few minutes earlier Charles
Cross, a horse-cart driver on his way to work, had passed the same spot, as had
Robert Paul, another horse-cart driver. They had both noted that the woman was
on her back with her skirt raised almost to her abdomen, but failed to see that her
throat had been cut and thought that she might just be dead drunk. They pulled
her skirt back down and went on their way to work vowing to tell the first

policeman they came across, which as it happened was Police Constable Jonas Mizen who they found on patrol in Hanbury Street.

Neil was joined by another officer, Police Constable John Thain who had passed Buck's Row at 3.30 a.m. and he verified that he had seen nobody at that time. Thain went to fetch local doctor, Rees Llewellyn. Mizen then arrived and was sent to collect an ambulance (which in those days was merely a trolley on which the body could be transported to the nearest mortuary). While waiting Neil made enquiries at properties in the immediate area, but nobody had heard or seen anything.

It was only when examined at the mortuary that the full extent of the injuries became known. In addition to almost severing the head, the abdomen had been ripped up, and the bowels were protruding. The abdominal wall, the whole length of the body, had been cut open, and on either side were two incised wounds almost as severe as the centre one. They reached from the lower part of the abdomen to the breast-bone.

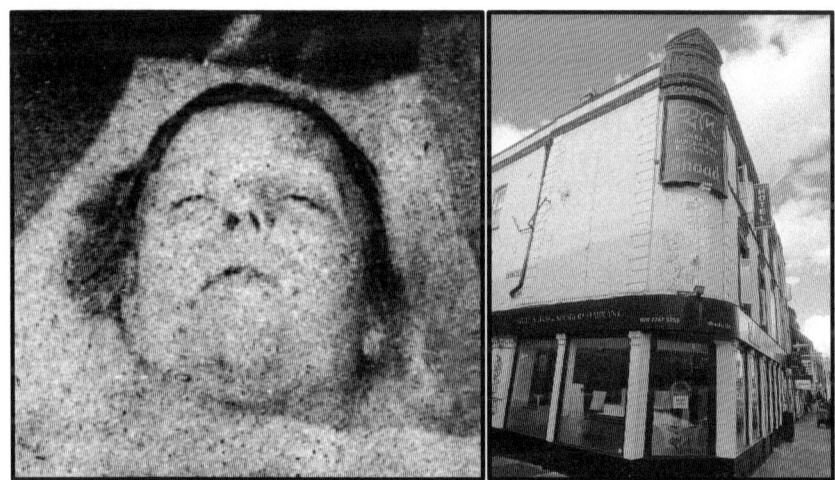

[Mortuary photograph of Mary Nichols (left), and the Frying Pan public house in 2021 (right)]

A local newspaper wrote that Dr Llewellyn had said that, 'she was ripped open just as you see a dead calf at the butcher's'. Even so these injuries were not as severe as those inflicted on later Jack the Ripper victims, which has led many to conclude that the killer was interrupted. It was also reported that the wounds had been inflicted by a left-handed person – a statement that Dr. Llewellyn was to later retract. Incredibly, up to that point, it was thought possible that the victim had committed suicide by cutting her own throat.

The next step was the identification of the body. The victim was 5 feet 2 inches tall, had a small scar on her forehead, 3 missing teeth (some reports claim 5), brown hair that was turning grey, a dark complexion, and was middle-aged. Her possessions amounted to just a comb, a broken fragment of a mirror, and a white handkerchief. Her clothes included a reddish-brown Ulster coat, a newish brown linsey frock, 2 petticoats (with the mark of the Lambeth Workhouse in Prince's Road), a pair of men's boots and a new black straw bonnet trimmed with black velvet. It was not long before she was identified as being Mary Ann 'Polly' Nichols of No. 18 Thrawl Street (a common lodging house). She had an estranged husband, William Nichols, whom she had married in 1864 and by whom she had had 5 children. He was able to add that she was actually 43-years old.

Polly's movements prior to her murder are well documented. It had been cold for the time of year, and raining frequently with some thunder and lightning. At 11.00 p.m. she had been seen walking (probably soliciting) in the Whitechapel Road and at around 12.30 a.m. she was spotted leaving the Frying Pan public house on the corner of Brick Lane and Thrawl Street. Polly was on her way back to the lodging house where around an hour later she was thrown out for not having the 4d. fee for the night.

Her last known appearance was in Osborn Street, where at the corner with Whitechapel Road, she met Emily Holland (a friend, fellow prostitute, and room-mate) with whom she spoke with for around 8 minutes. She told Emily that she had had her lodging money 3 times over that day but had spent it on drink – she appeared very drunk and staggered against a wall – but added that with her new bonnet she would have no trouble in finding a client and her doss money.

The prevalent theories were that Polly was murdered by a gang, a seaman, or a slaughterman/butcher. The police did their job diligently searching over 200 doss/common lodging houses and made 14 arrests, but all to no avail. On the 6th September Mary was buried at Manor Park Cemetery, Forest Gate. All would have been forgotten if there had not been another similar murder under two days later …

ANNIE CHAPMAN, LIVERPOOL STREET/ALDGATE EAST

The second Jack the Ripper body was to be found in the back yard of No. 29 Hanbury Street. The victim was another prostitute (and also a sieve-maker, who in addition earned money from crochet work, making antimacassars, and selling flowers) by the name of Annie Chapman, though also known as Annie Siffey, Annie Sivvy, and 'Dark Annie'.

[Coverage of the Annie Chapman murder in *The Illustrated Police News*. Note that they considered this the 4th killing in Whitechapel]

Annie was 47-years old, 5 feet tall with dark brown hair and a large thick nose. She was wearing a black figured jacket, brown bodice, black skirt, and lace boots. Her health was poor. She had been given medication for what was thought to be lung disease from which it is estimated she would have a life expectancy of just a few months. She was married to John Chapman, a coachman, by whom she had had 3 children. He had died in 1886 and since then she had been living at a common lodging house at No. 30 Dorset Street with the sieve-maker for whom she worked.

As with Polly Nichols (see page 95), Annie's last movements are well documented. At 2 a.m. she had spoken with Timothy Donovan, the deputy of a lodging house at No. 35 Dorset Street, and just like Polly she was drunk, and being without money to pay for a bed for the night was asked to leave. However, she was equally confident that she would return later. A John Richardson of No. 2 John Street was sitting on the steps leading to the backyard where Annie's body was found at around 4.45 a.m. and saw nothing.

A little later Albert Cadosch who lived next door at No. 27 Hanbury Street went into his backyard (which was separated from No. 29 by a fence 5 feet in height) and heard voices, but could not make any part of the conversation out except the word 'No'. He went out again at 5.28 a.m. as he heard a noise as if something was falling against the fence, and 2 minutes later a Mrs. Elizabeth Long saw a man and a woman (almost certainly Annie) in Hanbury Street close to The Alma public house. She was able to describe the man as being foreign, with dark hair and wearing a deerstalker hat and a dark overcoat – overall he was of 'shabby-genteel' appearance. Finally, at 6 a.m. John Davis, a resident at No. 29, was to discover Annie's body close to the back steps and partition fence.

Her injuries were vividly described by the *East London Observer* – 'a woman lay there with her clothes so disarranged as to expose her knees drawn up as if in agony, together with the lower portion of the abdomen, which had been mutilated in a frightful manner, the intestines, with the viscera and the heart, having been literally torn out of the mangled body and laid by her side. The head of the woman was turned back, revealing an enormous gash, so broad and so deep as almost to have severed the connection with the body. The face – that of a woman of about 40 – was deadly white, and the hair, which was wavy brown, was slightly disarranged. Portions of the flesh on the lower part of the body hung in shreds, the dress was bespattered with blood – as, indeed, was a portion of the fencing, as if it had received a spurt from a severed artery – beside the woman two pools of blood had formed, and upon her shoulders were slashes of blood and some of the viscera. Her head was lying towards the house, and her feet towards the end of the yard'. What was not mentioned was that part of the belly wall, the womb, the upper part of the vagina and the greater part of the bladder were all missing. She had also been partially strangulated – no doubt to make her unconscious while her dissection was performed. In addition, her wedding and keeper (designed to be close fitting and worn on a finger to stop another more valuable ring from slipping off) rings were missing, having been pulled from her fingers.

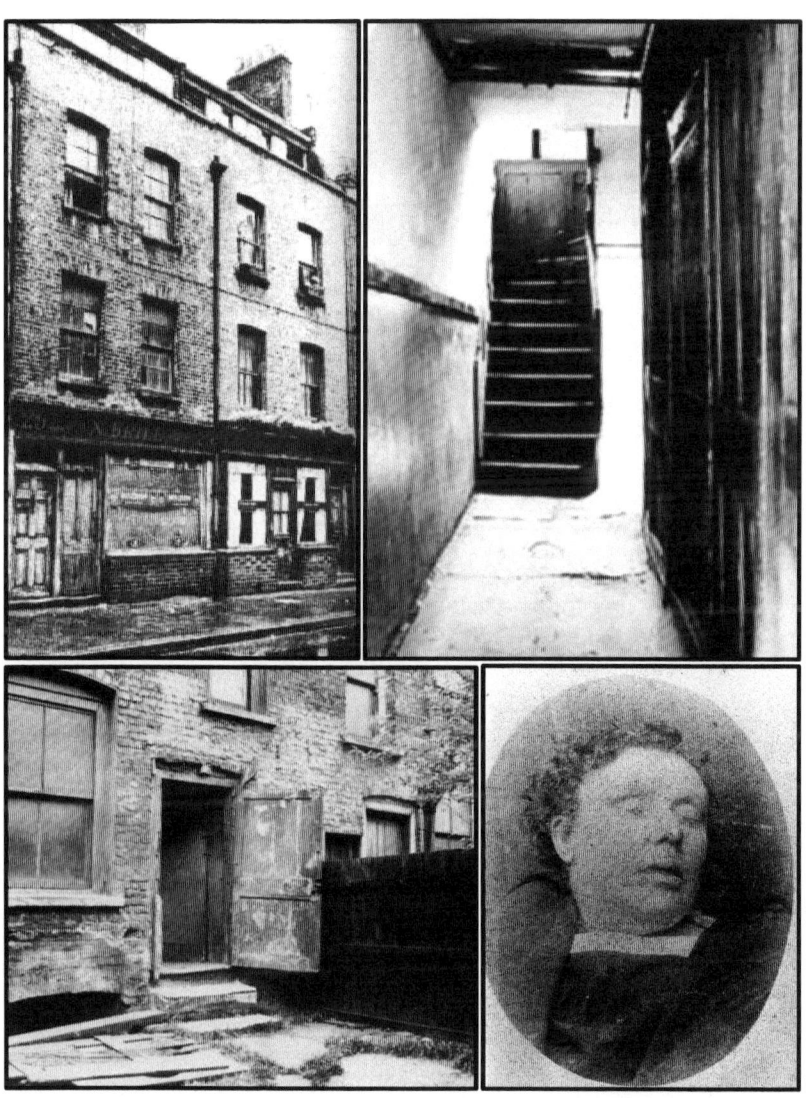

[Contemporary photographs of the murder site at No. 29 Hanbury Street along with the mortuary photograph of Annie Chapman]

The conclusions were that both Nichols and Chapman were killed by the same person who possessed some anatomical knowledge, and who latterly wanted to keep some body parts as a sort of trophy. It was also thought that the murder weapon was something like a small, narrow amputating knife, or possibly an implement such as would be used by a slaughterman, of about 6-8 inches in length.

[Today the location of where No. 29 Hanbury Street once stood is occupied by shops built into the edifice of the old Truman Brewery]

Having been removed by handcart to the mortuary in Montagu Street, Marylebone, Annie was subsequently buried on the 14th September in a communal grave at Manor Park Cemetery, Forest Gate – the same resting ground as Polly Nichols. The inquest into her death, which took place at the Working Lad's Institute in Whitechapel, commenced on the 10th September and was to last 5 days with the final day adjourned until the 26th September after her funeral. The inevitable verdict was that of wilful murder by person or persons unknown.

On the day of the murder the police acted swiftly: Several officers were placed on plain-clothes duty, interviews were conducted with all the inhabitants of No. 29 Hanbury Street as well as the adjoining houses, common lodging houses in the area were visited to see if anybody had arrived there with blood about their person, pawnbrokers and jewellers visited to see if Annie's missing rings could be traced, public houses visited to get more information about Annie's last movements and any of her clients that night, information circulated about possible suspects etc.

From the 15th September the police investigation was to be under the sole control of Chief Inspector Donald Swanson by order of Sir Charles Warren, the Metropolitan Police Commissioner.

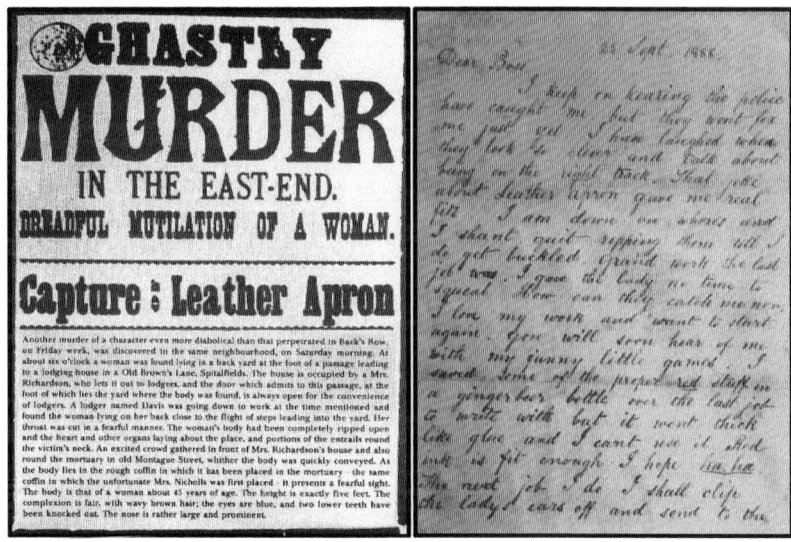

[A 'Leather Apron' poster (left) and the first 'Dear Boss' letter (right)]

As well as normal police enquiries there was also a 'red herring' in the form of a leather apron found in the backyard at No. 29 Hanbury Street with which to contend. It actually belonged to John Richardson, but at the time it fuelled speculation in the press, first mentioned in connection with the murder of Nichols, that the murderer was someone who used a leather apron for work, and most likely of Jewish origin. The hunt for 'Leather Apron' was afoot. One unfortunate individual named John Piser (in some documents Pizer), a 38-year old Polish Jew who made boots from leather (and was known locally as 'Leather Apron') was arrested on the 10th September. In fact, on the same day as Piser was arrested the police had 7 other suspects in detention. The fact that Piser had 'a cruel and sardonic look', used knives in his work, and used to be taunted by children was enough to make him an immediate suspect despite his having alibis for the nights in question. The accusation was so libellous that he was later able to get compensation from the newspaper that had named him as the prime suspect in the Whitechapel murders.

Suspects were plentiful and included William Piggott (a ship's cook), Friedrich Schumacher, Edward McKenna (an itinerant pedlar), Jacob Isenschmidt (a mentally ill man who had been a pork butcher), Oswald Puckeridge (another mentally ill man who had had surgical training, and who had recently been released from an asylum), and an unknown American physician who in 1887 (and probably later in 1888) had offered £20 per fresh body organ i.e. not one that had been preserved in alcohol.

Many suspects were arrested and released because the police still had no firm evidence as to who the murderer was, though they were soon to have his name, for on the 27th September the Central News Agency was to receive the first 'Dear Boss' letter signed 'Jack the Ripper' (which was not published until after the 'double event' of the 30th September 1888 – see page 105). In it he wrote of 'that joke about Leather Apron gave me the fits'. The name of Jack the Ripper was to stick thereafter. In fact, current thinking is that the 'Dear Boss' letter was a fake sent by a reporter, being written by an educated person trying to give the impression of being an illiterate one.

The police advised that prostitutes should walk in pairs, and carry whistles. Further they placed an extra 27 plain-clothes officers on the beat and drafted in other officers as from 1st October. There were also suggestions that Scotland Yard should disguise men as women prostitutes, have boxers dressed as women and with steel collars, and that the eyes of the victims should be photographed (in the belief that the retina captured and retained the last image the victims saw).

The police were doing all that they could but were being hampered, for as Sir Charles Warren reported in a letter to the Home Office, 'moreover the reporters for the press are following our detectives about everywhere in search of news and cross examine all parties interviewed so that they impede police action greatly'. He also stated his frustration that, 'no progress has as yet been made in obtaining any definite clue to the Whitechapel murders. A great number of clues have been examined and exhausted without finding any thing suspicious. A large staff of men are employed and every point is being examined which seems to offer any prospect of a discovery'.

The press were becoming increasingly unkind to the police with allegations of incompetence at every level. The Minister of Parliament for Whitechapel, Samuel Montagu, wanted to offer a £100 reward for information, but was refused permission by the Home Secretary, and in desperation some locals set up the Whitechapel Vigilance Committee.

The police with all their extra officers might well have thought that they were prepared for any further atrocity … but they were to be proved spectacularly wrong on the 30th September 1888 – the day of the 'double event'.

ELIZABETH STRIDE, ALDGATE EAST

[Various drawings of the Elizabeth Stride murder as featured in
The Illustrated Police News]

The 3rd canonical victim of Jack the Ripper was Elizabeth Stride (maiden name Elizabeth Gustafsdotter), also known as 'Long Liz' on account of her height/long legs. She was destined to meet her end at 1.00 a.m. in Dutfield's Yard, No. 40 Berner Street (now Henriques Street) which was adjacent to the International Working Men's Educational Club (IWMEC). The IWMEC is long gone having been replaced by the Harry Gosling Primary School – the murder spot is somewhere towards the middle of the playground.

Elizabeth was Swedish by birth but spoke almost perfect English and Yiddish, was 44-years old, had been married to a carpenter named John Stride, and apart from cleaning and other domestic work supplemented her income through prostitution. Elizabeth had run a coffee shop in Upper North Street, and later in Poplar High Street while living with her husband in East India Dock Road. However, after her marriage broke down in 1877 she had been an inmate at the Poplar workhouse before moving to a common lodging house at No. 32 Flower and Dean Street.

Unfortunately, Elizabeth was a bit of a fantasist, so much of what is reported about her may be false e.g. she claimed to have had 9 children though she is only known to have had one stillborn child in 1865. She also stated, maybe out of pride, that her husband and children had drowned in the *Princess Alice* disaster of 1878, when, in fact, John Stride was to die of heart disease in Bromley some 6 years later. More recently she had been living in Devonshire Street with Michael Kidney, a waterside labourer, but seems to have parted company with him since on the 27th September 1888 she was back at the common lodging house in Flower and Dean Street.

[Berner Street, now Henriques Street, showing the entrance to Dutfield's Yard – where the wheel is affixed to the wall of the building (top and bottom left), and the same site in 2020 – the body was found in what is now the middle of the school playground (bottom right)]

On the night of her death Elizabeth was seen drinking in the Queen's Head public house at around 6.30 p.m. with Elizabeth Tanner, the deputy at the lodging house.

She was wearing an old black skirt, black jacket trimmed with fur and with a posy of a red rose in a spray with either a fern or asparagus leaves pinned to it, a checked neckerchief, and a black crêpe bonnet.

[Contemporary illustration of the common lodging house in Flower and Dean Street where Elizabeth Stride resided (top left), which today would have stood just past the large iron gates on the left-hand side of what is now Lolesworth Street (bottom), and a Victorian photograph of another common lodging house in Flower and Dean Street (top right)]

There were 3 other possible sightings of her with clients in Berner Street around 11.00 p.m., 11.45 p.m., and 12.45 a.m. respectively. The last witness was Israel Schwartz who said that he had seen a man speaking to a woman in the gateway of the IWMEC and that the man had thrown the woman down onto the pavement. There was also another man across the street lighting a pipe, and when the attacker saw this person he shouted out 'Lipski'. Not wishing to get involved he had run away from the scene. Finally, 10 minutes earlier Police Constable William Smith had seen Elizabeth with a man opposite the IWMEC.

By midnight many of the members had left the IWMEC, with only around 20-30 remaining to talk and sing. There was no light in the yard. Elizabeth's body was found by the IWMEC's steward, Louis Diemschutz, who lived on the premises, but had been out that evening. He returned at 1.00 a.m., and as he drove his pony and cart into the yard he came across a 'bundle on the ground' by the gateway which upon inspection was found to be Elizabeth's body. The alarm was raised and soon the police were at the scene. All the IWMEC members still present were searched and had their statements taken. Others who had been there earlier in the evening were also interviewed, but none had seen a body as late as 12.50 a.m. on the morning in question.

Excerpts from the police surgeon's report stated that 'the body was lying on the near side, with the face turned toward the wall, the head up the yard and the feet toward the street. The left arm was extended and there was a packet of cachous (lozenges to mask bad breath) in the left hand … The right arm was over the belly; the back of the hand and wrist had on it clotted blood. The legs were drawn up with the feet close to the wall. The body and face were warm and the hand cold. The legs were quite warm … The throat was deeply gashed, and there was an abrasion of the skin about one and a quarter inches in diameter, apparently stained with blood, under her right brow. … There was a clear-cut incision on the neck. It was six inches in length and commenced two and a half inches in a straight line below the angle of the jaw, three quarters of an inch over an undivided muscle, and then, becoming deeper, dividing the sheath. The cut was very clean and deviated a little downwards …'.

It was concluded that she had been pulled backwards and onto the ground by her neckerchief, the knot of which was tight, before having her throat cut with a single slash as she was pinned to the ground. However, the injuries lacked the gruesomeness of those of Annie Chapman (see page 98) so it is thought that Jack the Ripper was disturbed, and did not have enough time to complete his work. Some claim that this was not a Jack the Ripper murder for (a) there was a lack of injuries, (b) it was the only murder committed south of the Whitechapel Road, and (c) the police surgeon's report established that the wounds were from a knife with a shorter blade than had been used previously.

Elizabeth was buried the following Saturday at the East London Cemetery, Plaistow.

Following the murder the police did their best against hostility from newspapers and other quarters. In today's terms they were hampered by 'the management of ignorance', the investigation was producing too many avenues of enquiry with witness statements often contradicting each other. Chief Inspector Swanson reported that 80,000 leaflets appealing for public information relating to Elizabeth's death had been distributed, and that in just one strand of the investigation, around 2,000 lodgers had been interviewed. The police desperately needed to prioritise their lines of enquiry, rather than trying to follow up on every lead. Matters were not made any easier when there was a second murder that morning …

CATHERINE EDDOWES, ALDGATE

[Drawings from *The Illustrated Police News* and *The Penny Illustrated Paper* covering the murder of Catherine Eddowes]

Like Elizabeth Stride (see page 105), Catherine Eddowes was also living at a common lodging house at Flower and Dean Street (No. 55). As well as Eddowes, she used the surname Kelly (after her current partner John Kelly) and Thomas Conway (after her ex-partner with whom she had had 3 children). She was 46-years old and one of 11 children herself, and although John Kelly claimed that Catherine was not a prostitute all the evidence points to her being one (occasional or otherwise), though both of them had just returned from paid work hop-picking in Kent the previous Thursday. She was originally from Birmingham and had a reputation for being both cheerful and singing all the time, as well as having a fierce temper. Catherine was 5 feet tall, with dark auburn hair and hazel eyes.

[A contemporary photograph of the south-west corner of Mitre Square where the body of Catherine Eddowes was found (top) and looking along the south side of the square in 2020 (bottom)]

On the 29th September Catherine told John that she was going over to see her daughter Annie Phillips who lived in Bermondsey (south of the river) in an attempt to get some money since that she had earned hop-picking had already been spent. John was to pawn his boots so that he could afford a place in a common lodging house that night. It is not known whether Catherine made that journey, or was successful in obtaining any money, but her next sighting was at 8.30 p.m. that night when she was found drunk in Aldgate High Street by Police Constable Louis Robinson. Not being able to ascertain where she lived, he, along with another officer, took Catherine to Bishopsgate police station where she was placed in a cell until she was thought sober enough to leave. That was at 1.00 a.m. when the police station inspector ordered her to be released. Some references state that she was let go because the police officers had grown tired of her endless singing – this is pure speculation as there is no evidence to suggest that she was in any a fit state to sing.

At that time she gave her name as Mary Ann Kelly with an address in Fashion Street. It was noted that she was wearing a black straw bonnet trimmed with green and black velvet, a black cloth jacket with imitation fur, a chintz skirt with a pattern of daisies and golden lilies, a grey stuff petticoat, an old green alpaca skirt and another even older blue skirt underneath, a neckerchief of red gauze, and an apron. When she left the police station it was raining. She did not go in the direction of Flower and Dean Street (probably because she had no money for her lodging) but in the opposite direction toward the City. Three men saw her at 1.35 a.m. talking with another man at the entrance to Church Passage close to Mitre Square. It was the unfortunate Police Constable Edward Watkins who was to find her body some 10 minutes later in the southwest corner of the square.

There was a tea warehouse in the square but the night watchman, an ex-police officer himself, said he had seen and heard nothing, and neither had the night watchman at No. 5, or the off-duty police officer who resided at No. 3. Just after 2.00 a.m. Dr. Frederick Brown was at the scene and in his subsequent report he stated that, 'the body was on its back, the head turned to her left shoulder. The arms by the side of the body as if they had fallen there … The clothes drawn up above the abdomen. The thighs were naked … The throat cut across … below the throat was a neckerchief … The intestines were drawn out to a large extent and placed over the right shoulder – they were smeared over with some feculent matter. A piece of about two feet was quite detached from the body and placed between the body and the left arm, apparently by design. The lobe and auricle of the right ear were cut obliquely through. There was a quantity of clotted blood on the pavement on the left side of the neck round the shoulder and upper part of the arm, and fluid blood-coloured serum which had flowed under the neck to the right shoulder, the pavement sloping in that direction … The peritoneal lining was cut through on the left side and the left kidney carefully taken out and removed … I believe the perpetrator of the act must have had considerable knowledge of the position of the organs in the abdominal cavity and the way of removing them …

111

It required a great deal of knowledge to have removed the kidney and to know where it was placed. Such a knowledge might be possessed by one in the habit of cutting up animals. I think the perpetrator of this act had sufficient time ... It would take at least five minutes. ... I believe it was the act of one person.' As well as the missing kidney part of her apron was also absent.

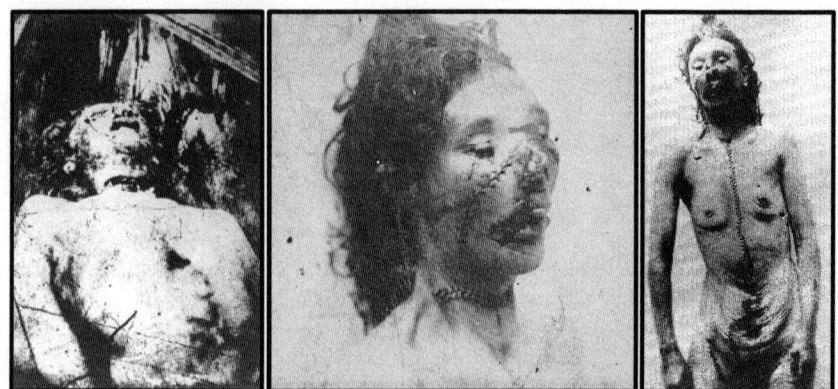

[Mortuary photographs of Catherine Eddowes]

Later Dr. Thomas Bond, the police physician (who was also involved with the Mary Kelly investigation – see page 115), was to disagree with the latter statements as to the murderer's skill level. He stated that, 'in each case the mutilation was inflicted by a person who had no scientific nor anatomical knowledge. In my opinion he does not even possess the technical knowledge of a butcher or horse slaughterer or any person accustomed to cut up dead animals'. Dr. William Saunders, the Public Analyst for the City of London, agreed in that he believed that Jack the Ripper was not looking to take any particular organ, and just happened upon the left kidney (and part of the womb) which were cut out with no significant anatomical skill.

The knife used was estimated to be one with a blade of 6 inches in length and therefore similar to that used in the Elizabeth Stride killing (see page 105). The murder was the first one not to take place in the East End, but within the bounds (just) of the City of London, and therefore under the jurisdiction of the City of London police (who had also placed extra patrols about the area). Hence the investigation was made in conjunction with the Metropolitan Police enquiries, and was to result in the production of some excellent crime scene drawings and plans of the vicinity. The general area was immediately searched with the result that at around 3.00 a.m. Police Constable Alfred Long found the missing fragment from Catherine's apron, stained with blood and faecal matter, lying in the passage of the doorway leading to Nos. 108 and 119 Model Dwellings, Goulston Street,

Whitechapel. Above it on the wall, and written in chalk, were the words, 'The Juwes are The men that Will not be Blamed for nothing'.

[The Model Dwellings in Goulston Street with shops below (left) and what used to be the entrance where the graffito was written in chalk, and also where the missing fragment of apron was found (right)]

This is known to 'Ripperologists' as the Goulston Street graffito, and is perceived as a vital clue, and one which upon the orders of Sir Charles Warren (at the suggestion of Police Superintendent Thomas Arnold) was washed away before being photographed. The reason given was that with dawn approaching the police did not want to incite a riot in this mainly Jewish district, especially at a time when tensions were at a peak.

By the 2nd October the police had pieced together from various interviews a general description of Jack the Ripper as being 'of shabby appearance, about 30 years of age and 5 feet 9 inches in height, of fair complexion, having a small fair moustache and a cap with a peak'.

113

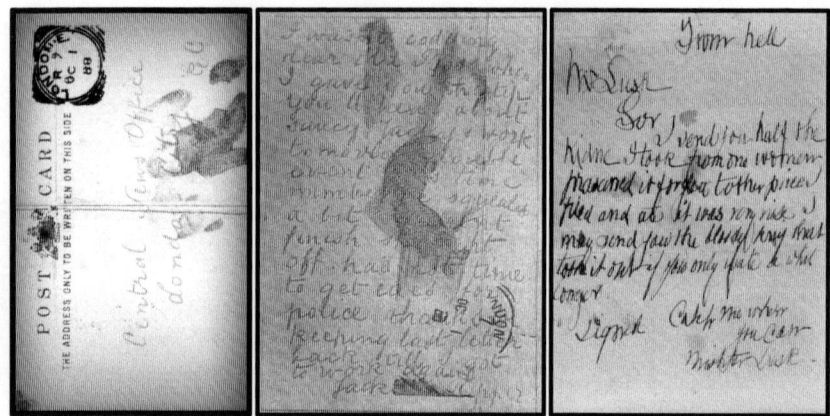

[The 'Saucy Jack' postcard (left and centre), and 'From Hell' letter (right)]

The newspapers were quick to criticise the police efforts, and the general public flooded the police with letters suggesting lines of enquiry that might be taken e.g. Jack the Ripper escapes via the sewers, he disguises himself as a policeman, that a gang might be responsible, the murderer is a watchman etc. Jack the Ripper also wrote his famous 'Saucy Jack' postcard sent on the 1st October 1888. Like the 'Dear Boss' letter a few days earlier (see page 104) it was viewed as being a fraud, but it did not stop the newspapers publishing both of them (and in so doing increasing their circulation) – the only real effect publication had was that it led to other hoax letters being sent which were to take up valuable police time and resources.

On the 16th October George Lusk, the chairman of the Whitechapel Vigilance Committee, received the 'From Hell' letter along with a portion of a human kidney – the other half, the letter claimed, had been eaten by Jack the Ripper. At first it was thought that the letter was genuine for the kidney did match the one missing from Catherine's body i.e. had the correct length of renal artery where it had been severed, and had Bright's disease. However, later evidence shows that the kidney had been trimmed, the renal artery was entirely absent, and it had been placed in preservative – the conclusion was that the kidney had been obtained from a hospital morgue and been sent, most likely, by a medical student as a prank.

Catherine was buried on the 8th October in the City of London Cemetery in Manor Park.

In the weeks that followed the police continued their investigations much as before, only with even more men at their disposal. More leaflets were printed, a reward of £500 was now offered from the Corporation of the City of London, the two police forces had daily meetings, various properties were searched, arrests made, suspects interviewed, patrols stepped up to a frequency of every 15 minutes, and even two bloodhounds (Barnaby and Burgho) were assessed over 2 days in Regent's Park and Hyde Park for their ability to follow a scent should another murder occur. The newspapers were now even more critical of the police, running headlines such as *The Headless Criminal Investigation Department* and *Why Detectives Don't Detect*. Mitre Square, in particular, was becoming a tourist attraction with sightseers wanting to view where the murder took place. Some 4,000 women signed a petition to Queen Victoria, and the police received 1,500 letters of help along with some confessions. Even Sir Arthur Conan Doyle, the creator of Sherlock Holmes, was asked for his opinion/expertise.

In a letter written on the 23rd October 1888 to the Home Secretary, Robert Anderson (who was by then the head of the CID as well as being the Assistant Commissioner) expresses his frustration thus: 'I wish to guard against its being supposed that the inquiry is now concluded ... that a crime of this kind should have been committed without any clue being supplied by the criminal, is unusual, but that 5 (he was including the murder of Martha Tabram on the 7th August 1888 who today is not thought to have been a Jack the Ripper victim) successive murders should have been committed without our having the slightest clue of any kind is extraordinary, if not unique, in the annals of crime. The result has been to necessitate our giving attention to innumerable suggestions, such as would in any ordinary case be dismissed unnoticed ... moreover, the activity of the Police has been to a considerable extent wasted through the exigencies of sensational journalism, and the action of unprincipled persons, who, from various motives, have endeavoured to mislead us. But on the other hand the public generally and especially the inhabitants of the East End have shown a remarkable desire to assist in every way, even at some sacrifice to themselves ... the vigilance of the officers engaged on the inquiry continues unabated'.

October came and went without incident, but then just as some thought that the Jack the Ripper attacks were over ...

MARY KELLY, LIVERPOOL STREET/ALDGATE EAST

The death of Mary Kelly was different from the previous 4 murders and some 'Ripperologists' believe that it should not be attributed to Jack the Ripper. For a start Mary was far younger than the other victims at just 25-years old. It was also the only murder to take place indoors (at No. 13 Miller's Court at the back of No. 26 Dorset Street, Spitalfields where she lived), and it took place over 5 weeks after the previous murder with the mutilations being far in excess of anything seen thus far.

115

[Coverage of the Mary Kelly murder as printed in *The Illustrated Police News* who considered her the 7th victim of Jack the Ripper]

Mary, who also went by the names Marie Jeanette, 'Fair' Emma, 'Ginger', 'Dark' Mary and 'Black' Mary, was born in Ireland (probably Limerick) but like Elizabeth Stride (see page 105) was prone to flights of fantasy. Hence, she may/may not have lived in Wales where she married a coal miner named Davis or Davies, been disowned by her parents, come from a moderately wealthy family, had 7 brothers and a sister, had a family member on the London theatrical stage, been well educated, and was/was not a good artist.

She was reported as being a blonde, or a redhead – which rather contradicts her being known as 'Black' Mary or 'Ginger' – 5 feet 7 inches in height, slim, attractive and with a fresh complexion. The 'Dark' Mary title comes from the fact that while resident in the East End she took to drinking heavily after which she would start to sing Irish songs and become generally abusive and unpleasant.

In approximately 1884 she moved to London and worked in Chelsea, and Fitzrovia in the West End, where she became a high-class prostitute working out of a brothel. Mary was very popular and one client even took her to France.

Afterwards she adopted the French name Marie Jeanette. However, there must have been a downturn in her life, for a year later she was to be found in the East End, lodging in the Ratcliffe Highway (see page 35), and later in Stepney (see page 23), before ending up at a lodging house in Thrawl Street, Spitalfields (see page 69). It was here she met, and became partner to, a fish porter at Billingsgate Market called Joseph Barnett. They lived together in George Street, then Little Paternoster Row, followed by a period in Brick Lane (see page 169) before finally settling in Dorset Street in early 1888. At the time of her murder Mary and Joseph were not together, having argued a week before about Mary letting other prostitutes use their dwelling – there was also friction between them because Joseph had recently lost his job which forced Mary back onto the streets.

On the evening of the 8th September 1888 it was raining hard. Joseph visited Mary at Miller's Court at around 7.00 p.m. and found her with Maria Harvey. They were joined by another prostitute, Lizzie Albrook, before Joseph and Maria left together. At that time Mary was sober, but later in the evening she was seen in the company of Elizabeth Foster at the Ten Bells public house on the corner of Commercial Street and Fournier Street, Spitalfields, and later still with 2 other people at the Horn of Plenty public house in Dorset Street. Mary Cox, another prostitute and resident at No. 5 Miller's Court, saw her return drunk to Miller's Court at 11.45 p.m. with a man/client.

[Mary Kelly by her lodging at Miller's Court – note the broken window pane (left), and the Ten Bells public house (right)]

117

[The entrance to Miller's Court (top left), and Mary Kelly's abode at No. 13 Miller's Court (top right), and the same redeveloped locations in 2020 showing the Spitalfields Fruit & Wool Exchange building (bottom left), and the atrium (bottom right)]

Kelly could be heard singing in her room as late as 1.00 a.m., but by 1.30 a.m. the singing, according to Elizabeth Prater who lived directly above, had stopped. Elizabeth also said that she (corroborated by Sarah Lewis who was sleeping at No. 2 Miller's Court) heard a faint cry of 'Murder' between 3.30 a.m. and 4.00 a.m. but had taken no notice of it at the time since such cries were common in the area. Cox also thought that she heard somebody leaving Mary's room at 5.45 a.m.

There was a separate sighting of Mary at 2.00 a.m. by a man named George Hutchinson who stated that he met Mary at Flower and Dean Street, after which she went off in the direction of Thrawl Street where she was approached by a wealthy-looking man of Jewish appearance. Hutchinson was suspicious of this person who looked so out of place in the area. Consequently, he kept watch on them both until 2.45 a.m. at which point they had been inside No. 13 Miller's Court for some time. Once again, Sarah Lewis was able to partially verify these latter movements as she confirmed seeing a drunk man and women in the courtyard at 2.30 a.m.

On the morning of the 9th November it was still raining which was a pity for all those involved in the Lord Mayor's Show that day. It was going to be a day to remember for Thomas Bowyer, an assistant to Mary Kelly's landlord John McCarthy, when he was sent around to No. 13 Miller's Court to collect the rent arrears (6 weeks). It was just after 10.45 a.m. when he knocked on the door to no reply. Not being deterred, he then pushed aside the clothing covering a broken windowpane and saw the mutilated body of Mary on the bed.

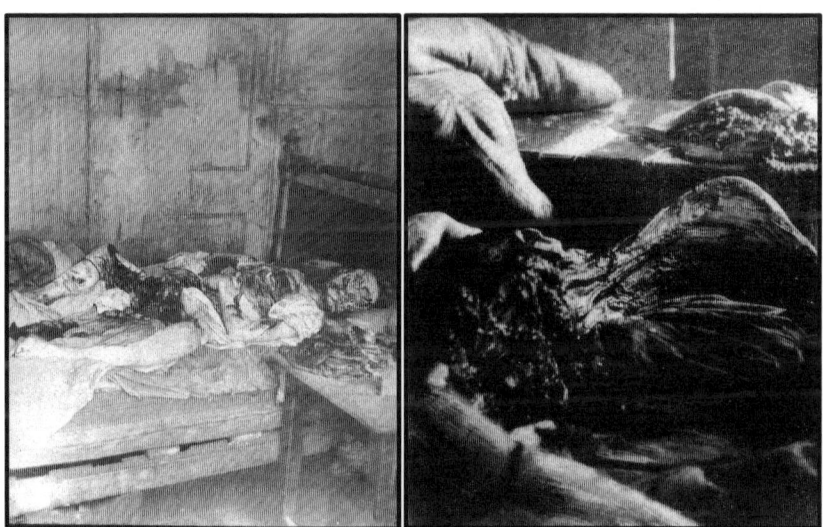

[The 2 crime scene photographs taken of Mary Kelly]

The police were called and were soon on the scene, among them were Police Superintendent Thomas Arnold, Police Inspector Edmund Reid, Police Inspector Frederick Abberline (who had been seconded to Whitechapel from the Central Office at Scotland Yard after the murder of Polly Nichols – see page 95), and Assistant Commissioner Robert Anderson. The bloodhounds Barnaby and

119

Burgho (see page 115) were called for but by now the scent had gone cold. It was noted that women's clothes had been burnt in the fireplace, presumably to give more light for Jack the Ripper to carry out his mutilations – the only other form of light in the room at night-time being a single candle. News travelled fast and it is estimated 1,000 people soon gathered in Dorset Street, with many of them voicing their disapproval of the police investigation to date.

Two crime scene photographs were taken and the body removed via a horse-drawn wagon to the mortuary in Shoreditch. This time the body was examined jointly by Dr. Thomas Bond (who was also involved with the Catherine Eddowes murder – see page 109) and Dr. Bagster Phillips. The mutilations were so severe that Phillips suggested that it would have taken Jack the Ripper 2 hours to complete, though he did not believe that the person responsible showed any signs of medical or anatomical training. The implement used was a knife, around 6 inches long and 1 inch wide, a statement which is in accord with the knife used in the previous murders.

The subsequent post-mortem stated that 'The body was lying naked in the middle of the bed ... the legs were wide apart, the left thigh at right angles to the trunk and the right forming an obtuse angle with the pubis. The whole of the surface of the abdomen and thighs was removed and the abdominal cavity emptied of its viscera. The breasts were cut off, the arms mutilated by several jagged wounds and the face hacked beyond recognition of the features. The tissues of the neck were severed all round down to the bone. The viscera were found in various parts viz. the uterus and kidneys with one breast under the head, the other breast by the right foot, the liver between the feet, the intestines by the right side and the spleen by the left side of the body. The flaps removed from the abdomen and thighs were on a table. The bed clothing at the right corner was saturated with blood, and on the floor beneath was a pool of blood covering about two feet square ... The face was gashed in all directions, the nose, cheeks, eyebrows, and ears being partly removed. The lips were blanched and cut by several incisions running obliquely down to the chin. There were also numerous cuts extending irregularly across all the features ... Both breasts were more or less removed by circular incisions, the muscle down to the ribs being attached to the breasts ...'. In fact, unlike the other victims, it was remarked that Mary's body had not been ripped open, but sliced.

The inquest at Shoreditch Town Hall produced no new evidence, though in his report Dr. Bond did give a profile of the type of person the police were looking for as being a 'quite likely inoffensive looking man probably middle-aged and neatly and respectably dressed. I think he must be in the habit of wearing a cloak or overcoat or he could hardly have escaped notice in the streets if the blood on his hands and clothes were visible'. It was this statement more than any other that has given rise to the image of Jack the Ripper being a gentleman in a top hat with a cloak and cane. Dr. Bond further said that the perpetrator was most likely a solitary, eccentric individual who was subject to periodic attacks of homicidal and erotic mania, who had been in an extreme state of satyriasis as he performed his mutilations.

Mary was buried on the 19th November 1888 at St. Patrick's Roman Catholic Cemetery in Leytonstone. The inscription on her grave reads, 'In loving memory of Marie Jeanette Kelly. None but the lonely hearts can know my sadness. Love lives forever'.

The police investigation included extensive questioning of both Joseph Barnett and George Hutchinson (both of whom were regarded as prime suspects) as well as door-to-door searches. A pardon was even offered for anybody who might be considered an accomplice if they came forward with the identity of Jack the Ripper. Sir Charles Warren was also to resign, not over the Whitechapel murders *per se* but over articles he had written attacking government interference in what he considered were police matters. Although he was disliked by the press and the politicians, he was respected by his own men, with virtually every police superintendent on the force visiting him at home to express their support and regret at his departure.

Queen Victoria spoke for many when she was moved to write to the Prime Minister, 'This new most ghastly murder shows the absolute necessity for some very decided action. All these courts must be lit, and our detectives improved. They are not what they should be. You promised, when the first murder took place, to consult with your colleagues about it'.

Many references claim that the police investigation was downsized following Mary's death, but the opposite is true. There were 143 plain-clothes officers involved in the investigation in November and December 1888 (over 100 more officers than in September that year). Taking in all ranks the Whitechapel Division had 585 men on call. It was only after there had been no more victims that the number of police was reduced in the New Year.

As if to prove this point in his end of year report James Monro, who had taken over as Commissioner after the resignation of Sir Charles Warren, stated, 'The agitation which centred in Trafalgar Square, and the murders in Whitechapel, necessitated the concentration in particular localities of large bodies of police, and such an increase of force in one quarter of the Metropolis, it must be remembered, is only procurable by diminishing the number of men ordinarily employed in other divisions'. He went on to complain that because of the extra men in Whitechapel that the consequence was 'diminished numbers of police in other quarters, and so long as the available force is hardly sufficient, as it is just now, for the

121

performance of the ordinary and every day duties of the Police, and an additional drain on its resources leads to a diminished protection against, and consequent increase of, crime'. In his view the police were 'overworked, and under such circumstances crime cannot be met or coped with in a satisfactory and efficient manner'. Finally, with reference to Jack the Ripper specifically he reported his regret that 'in spite of most strenuous efforts on the part of the Police, the criminal has up till now remained undiscovered'.

And that for most 'Ripperologists' was the last of Jack the Ripper. Over the years since 1888 suspects have come and gone, and it is probable that the true identity of Jack the Ripper will never be known. However, if you wish to find out more about other possible victims, the suspects, and a new theory then our sister publication *In The Footsteps Of Jack The Ripper* is recommended. It even includes 2 fully illustrated Jack the Ripper tours that you can take to investigate the area in more detail.

13. A DOUBLE KILLING IN AMHURST ROAD HACKNEY CENTRAL (1893)

The first of the double killings in this book is a story of change, a story of how Thomas Morgan, a quiet, unassuming, middle-aged, respectable man who ran a coffee house and lodging at No. 17 Amhurst Road could change into a double murderer.

[*The Illustrated Police News* coverage of the Thomas Morgan case]

Thomas had been a widower until 1889 when he married Emma Jennings, herself a widow with several grown-up children and a 10-year-old son named Arthur Jennings from her previous marriage. Together the 3 of them ran Morgan's Coffee House successfully, but this changed in the summer of 1892 when Thomas had a stroke which was to affected his speech and paralysed the right side of his body. As is common with such strokes his personality was affected also. He became an angry and offensive man who now resented his stepson, and often his loving wife as well.

123

Events came to ahead on the night of the 23rd May 1893 when Thomas went to the room where Arthur was sleeping and shot him with a Smith & Wesson revolver. This woke Emma who went to see what the disturbance was – she was shot in the face. Thomas then went to his own room where he fired 2 more shots, one into his stomach and another into his groin, after which he pulled a bell-rope to summon the 2 young servant girls who worked for him in the coffee house. They sent for the police and a doctor.

Thomas was taken to the German Hospital in nearby Dalston and on the way made a confession to a police officer. Thomas himself died from his own injuries the following day. The verdict of the coroner's court was wilful murder by Thomas Morgan who had then committed suicide while mentally deranged.

[This parade of shops is where Thomas Morgan's coffee shop in Amhurst Road was located in 1893]

In the same year that Thomas Morgan murdered his wife and stepson, there was a second killing in the same street. This time the location was No. 53 Amhurst

124

Road where solicitor Solomon Myers lived with his wife and 5 children. The household employed 3 servants, one of whom, Emily Newber, was of German extraction.

[Postcard of Amhurst Road from the turn of the 20th century]

The 15-year old Emily was taken on as nursemaid to the Myers' 10-month old baby Ray Maud Myers on the 3rd December 1893. After just 5 days it was apparent that Ray was unwell. She had swollen lips and eyes along with scratches that had appeared on her face. After questioning all the servants, Mrs. Myers gave Emily, who had protested her innocence and accused the other 2 servants of injuring the baby, notice to leave. The following day it became clear that Ray had been further ill-treated when she was found in the presence of Emily with bloody lips and foaming at the mouth. In addition, Solomon noticed that there was a strong smell of vinegar (acetic acid) that led him to believe that Emily was deliberately trying to poison his daughter.

Upon more vigorous questioning Emily admitted striking Ray the previous day as she had been made angry by the baby's crying, but she flatly denied any other actions. A doctor was called and Ray was admitted to the German Hospital in Dalston. Here Dr. Zumbusch confirmed that Ray had been poisoned by a corrosive substance such as acetic acid that had made her throat swollen and burnt to the point where breathing was impaired. He successfully performed a tracheotomy but pneumonia set in and Ray died a few days later. The pneumonia was from the aspiration of the acetic acid and mucus. On further investigation an almost empty bottle of acetic acid that had been purchased for wart removal was found in the general servants' bedroom.

[The German Hospital in Dalston, circa 1864]

Emily was placed on trial at the Old Bailey for the wilful murder of Ray Myers. During the trial it was revealed that Emily had been dismissed from various other nursemaid positions, and newspapers reported that she had a hatred of Jews (having read that they drank blood of Christian children and were plotting to take over the world). A Dr. Gimblet testified that in his opinion Emily showed signs of having a homicidal mania given that she showed no remorse for what she had done. The jury returned a verdict of manslaughter but with a recommendation for mercy due to the prisoner's youth. Emily was sentenced to just 1 week in prison and 5 years in reformatory.

HACKNEY

[The Chapel of Ease, West Hackney, circa 1900, was opened in 1814. It was located at the junction of Amhurst Road and Stoke Newington Road, but was destroyed during World War II. The replacement church dedicated to St. Paul was opened in 1960]

The area of Hackney is thought by some to be derived from the Anglo-Saxon *haccan* meaning 'to kill with a sword or axe' and *ey* 'a river' indicating that some battle may have taken place here close to the river. Its main houses were on either side of the road running from Mile End to where it joins the main north road at Stamford Hill. One of its oldest buildings is the church of St. Augustine said to have been constructed by the Knights Templar in around 1300. Two notable residents were Edward de Vere (who some claim was the true author of Shakespeare's plays) and the founder of Charterhouse, Thomas Sutton. In the 19th century Hackney was still regarded as being largely rural in character with a population in 1801 of 12,730 persons. This changed with the coming of the railway and expansion of London such that a hundred years later the population was over 200,000 persons. Today it is an ethnically diverse area where some 89 languages are spoken according to the last census.

Perhaps the areas greatest claim to fame is the hackney carriage, better known as the taxicab the world over. The exact etymology of the hackney carriage is uncertain. Whereas most claim that it is derived from the fact that Hackney supplied horses from its surrounding meadows for horse-drawn carriages, it is also possibly a corruption of the French word *haquenée* (a medium-sized horse recommended for lady riders). What is known for certain is that the first hackney-carriage licenses in London date from an Act of Parliament in 1662 which allowed for a maximum of 400 such licenses to be issued for horse-drawn vehicles that were available for hire.

14. THE DOUBLE MURDER IN TURNER STREET WHITECHAPEL (1896)

Jonathan Levy was a miser who had made his money from the manufacture of umbrellas, but in 1896 was retired and living with his housekeeper, Annie Gale, at No. 31 Turner Street (on the corner with Varden Street). Turner Street runs between Whitechapel Road and Commercial Road, making its way between various buildings of the Royal London Hospital at its northern end.

[*Penny Illustrated Paper* drawings of the main characters in the murder of Annie Gale and Jonathan Levy by William Seaman (left), and the escape route through the ceiling from *The Illustrated Police News* (right)]

On the 4th April 1896 he was spotted leaving the house by a professional burglar called William Seaman. Taking his opportunity, Seaman rang the doorbell to see if anybody was at home. When Gale opened the door, Seaman forced his way into the house, and in the process beat her with a poker from the grate before cutting her throat with a knife. In fact, so violent was the attack that he nearly severed her head. He then set about searching for valuables which he put in his pockets. When Levy returned a few minutes later he received the same treatment as Gale. The attack on Levy was noisier and alerted a neighbour who called for help. Seaman needed to escape, but Levy had locked the front door behind him and Seaman could not find the key. Improvising, he took a hammer and knocked a hole in the bedroom ceiling to gain access to the roof. By now the police had entered the house and were soon also on the roof. The only option was to jump the 40 feet to the ground. Seaman survived, though he broke his right shoulder and injured his leg (and landed beside a small girl who received a concussion). The jump didn't help as he was immediately arrested.

[Artist impressions of the confrontation on the roof]

At trial Seaman, who defended himself, claimed that the police officers had lied, but this strategy was not successful and he was found guilty of the double murder, and hanged at Newgate Prison on the 9th June 1896.

[Today No. 31 Turner Street (left) looks nothing like it did at the time of the murder, though No. 33 opposite does give a good idea of the type of property in which Levy lived (right)]

ROYAL LONDON HOSPITAL

[Façade of the London Hospital, circa 1903]

At the time of opening in 1757 the London Hospital in Whitechapel Road was the finest in London, and remained so for at least 50 years (since there were no other London hospitals either built or refurbished until the 19th century). When its foundations were laid in 1753, it was in order to replace The London Infirmary, that had been founded in 1740 in Featherstone Street (Moorfields), and had itself moved to larger premises in Prescott Street (Aldgate) a year later.

In the early years, patients were classified as either being 'cured' or 'relieved', and if treatment was successful the patient upon discharge had to give thanks to the committee and 'their kind benefactors', and also go to their parish church to give thanks to God. If they failed in this undertaking they were put on a black list and never treated again.

The hospital grew rapidly with an east wing being added in 1775, followed by a west wing 3 years later. It was in the east wing that in 1785 Sir William Blizard and Thomas Maddocks co-founded the medical school. Its facilities included a chemical laboratory, museum, and dissecting room. This was a unique feature of the hospital and quite revolutionary for up until then all medical schools were private, and disassociated themselves from hospitals as much as possible, for the view held by the governors of the time was that hospitals were for the treating of 'poor objects' and not for the 'purpose of instruction'.

132

Another prominent person to be associated with the London Hospital was Dr. Thomas Barnardo who later became the founder of Dr. Barnardo's Homes for the care of vulnerable children.

[Helene Rachael ward at the London Hospital, circa 1910]

By 1876, when Queen Victoria opened a new hospital wing there were beds for nearly 800 patients, making the London Hospital the largest in the country. The following year a new Medical College, described as being 'the most convenient, salubrious and handsome school in the Metropolis', along with a Nurses' Home was opened by the Prince of Wales.

Probably the most famous patient of the hospital was Joseph Merrick (better known as 'The Elephant Man'), who lived here from 1886 until his death in 1890.

During World War II the building suffered extensive damage from enemy bombing, though the majority of the 18th- and 19th-century structure remained intact. Over the years there was extensive rebuilding, amalgamations (e.g. St. Clement's Hospital at Mile End was incorporated into the London Hospital, while the Medical School became part of the University of London), and additions (e.g. a new School of Physiotherapy was established in 1936, and the Alexandra Wing was added in 1982). In 1990, following a visit by the Queen to mark the hospital's 250th anniversary its official title was changed to the Royal London Hospital, and in the same year it also became home to London's Air Ambulance (the only emergency helicopter service in the Capital).

15. MURDER AT THE LORD NELSON PUBLIC HOUSE WHITECHAPEL (1903)

The Lord Nelson public house was situated at No. 145 (No. 299 in current numbering) Whitechapel Road (see page 77) and was typical of establishments of that era. On the night in question, the 23rd September 1903, it was due to close (as it always did) at half past midnight, and by quarter past the place was virtually empty. However, without warning Jerry Slowe, who was described as being a short, ugly, meanly dressed chap who fancied Martha Hardwick, the sister of the landlady Hannah Starkey, burst in and struck out at Martha who collapsed on the floor. Hannah jumped over the counter to give chase to Slowe who was now outside. She called out for help to her 2 potmen, Pealling and Musgrave, to 'catch him and kill him!'.

[The murder of Martha Hardwick by Jerry Stowe as covered in
The Illustrated Police News, September 1903]

Musgrave not being so light of foot soon gave up, but Pealling caught up with Slowe only to receive a blow to the jaw, but still he followed at a distance. His

135

perseverance was rewarded when he spotted a Police Constable (William Bowden) on duty and it was he who detained Slowe and marched him back to the Lord Nelson where Police Constable Hubert Haddock joined them. In fact, it was not a simple case of assault but one of murder, for Martha was lying in a pool of blood having been stabbed with a knife – the same implement that Slowe had dropped (and which was later recovered) in the street during the chase.

[The following month, October 1903, there was further coverage of the murder in *The Illustrated Police News*]

Slowe went to trial at the Old Bailey on the 19th October and was hanged at Pentonville Prison on the 10th November. It transpired that although he had been drunk at the time, the murder was not a spontaneous assault, but was very much a pre-meditated act since he had stolen the murder weapon from his employer earlier in the evening, and brought it with him with the intent to cause harm to Martha. He had been drinking at the Lord Nelson earlier in the evening, had left, loitered outside until nearly closing time when the place would be empty of customers, and then re-entered (but only when the lights were being turned off so he would not necessarily be recognised in the darkness).

Social reformers were keen to reduce the number of alcohol related crimes during the Edwardian period and as a consequence between 1900 and 1908 the number of public houses in Britain fell from 7,800 to 6,700 with the Lord Nelson being one of the casualties. Ironically, it became a prayer meeting house owned by the London City Mission.

[The site of the Lord Nelson is now a woman's clothes shop]

PUBLIC HOUSES AT THE TURN OF THE 20TH CENTURY

[Being served through the window in Whitechapel Road]

Over the past 250 years one thing that there has never been a shortage of in London are public houses. Towards the end of the 19th century around 900,000 people lived in the East End and of those around a quarter were in Whitechapel itself. They lived in common lodging houses, and overcrowded slums made up of courts and alleyways where more than one family might occupy a single room – many lived on the streets and most sought solace in the public houses. Alcohol, mainly in the form of gin, was widely available and cheap. A common advertising slogan of the time was 'Drunk for a penny, dead drunk for tuppence'.

The licensing laws allowed public houses to open up to $20^1/_2$ hours a day. In general, they were the first business to open in the morning, and the last to close in the early hours of the following morning. Only those under the age of 14 years could not be served. They were places where luxury and squalor, gilded affluence and shame-faced dinginess, stood side-by-side.

Premises close to markets (e.g. Covent Garden) would be the first to open at around 3 a.m., and were closely followed by establishments at the terminal railway stations. At this time the Metropolis had around 4,000 public houses. The West End was dominated by wine-houses where port was the favoured drink, while spirits were in high demand in the financial district close to the Bank of England. In the East End it was beer that was both produced and drunk in great quantity by the men, with gin the tipple of choice for the ladies.

Dirty Dick's, in Bishopsgate Street, had a policy of rigorously enforcing a rule which only allowed a customer a single drink per visit. The same was true at an adjacent hostelry in Artillery Lane which operated a 'one call, one cup' system, with a copy of the rules of the house being presented to each new customer. Another curious place was the Vine Tavern in the Mile End Road, a wooden building that stood detached and apart, like an island, in the middle of the road. Close by, in Whitechapel Road was London's only 'open bar' where customers stood on the pavement and were served from a pewter-topped window ledge.

[Petticoat Lane, one of 4 important markets in Spitalfields]

Many establishments, especially in the West End and financial district, only held 6-day licenses and had to close on a Sunday, though this was rarely strictly observed. Those that did open were only allowed to do so between 1 p.m. and 3 p.m., and then again between 6 p.m. and 11 p.m., unless the customer was a traveller who had journeyed more than 3 miles (but not for the express purpose of obtaining a drink) in which case they were permitted refreshment during closed hours. Many used this rule to their advantage by joining one of the numerous bicycle clubs that during the summer months would organise outings with frequent stops at public houses along their route. While this ploy may have worked at the Bull and Bush at Hampstead, in the East End there were few travellers of this sort. Here Petticoat Lane Market where 1,000s of people gathering to buy and sell clothes was the excuse. However, the landlords were strict, for fear of losing their license, and would only serve a customer who could produce a valid unused return half of a railway or bus ticket. As observed by one French visitor most London bus routes started/terminated either at railway stations or public houses.

Finally, a peculiarity of the English public house was that most were divided in the 'private' bar and the 'saloon' bar. Both charged the same prices, but customers who wished to escape the 'mutable many' would patronise the former. The saloon bar was for locals and their ladies who were mostly known to the landlord and who would address the barmaids by their first names. The saloon bar was often the ante-chamber to the billiard room.

16. The Houndsditch Murders
Liverpool Street/Aldgate (1910)

[Henry Harris' shop just after the murders with police keeping
watch outside (top), and the same location in 2021 (bottom)]

On the 16th December 1910 it was a jewellery shop owned by Henry Samuel
Harris, located at No. 119 Houndsditch, which became the scene of an attempted
robbery by a group of anarchists. The original intention of the gang was to rent
No. 10 Exchange Buildings, a tenement which was immediately behind their
target, but this was not available. Instead, they took both No. 9 and No. 11 (under
the names of Fritz Svaars and Joe Levi respectively) and brought in various pieces
of equipment they would need. This included 60 feet of India rubber gas hose, a
cylinder of compressed gas, and some diamond-tipped drills. If they had
succeeded in breaking in, they might have been disappointed with their haul, for
although it was thought that the shop held an estimated £20,000-£30,000 of stock
in the safe, Harris' son later confirmed that the safe only contained around £7,000
in merchandise.

[The original Bishopsgate police station designed by Sir Horace Jones (who was also responsible for Tower Bridge, Smithfield and Leadenhall Markets) dating from 1866 (left), and the current building constructed on the same site and opened in 1939 just prior to World War II during which it received a direct hit from enemy bombing raid, but due to it being structurally reinforced remained virtually undamaged (right)]

Max Weil, who ran an import business out of No. 120 Houndsditch, arrived home at around 10 p.m. that night to find his sister and housemaid in a state of agitation, since they had heard sounds emanating from the jewellers next door consistent with somebody trying to break in from the rear of the building i.e. from Exchange Buildings. As the good citizen that he was, Weil went to alert the police at the nearby Bishopsgate police station, and shortly afterwards returned with Police Constable Walter Piper who he found on the way. The policeman made a preliminary investigation and could hear the suspicious noises from outside No. 118 and No. 120 Houndsditch. At around 11 p.m. he knocked on the door of No. 11 Exchange Buildings (as it was the only property with a light on in the back) and spoke briefly to the man who came to the door. He acted in a furtive manner. Piper was not convinced by the man's answers and was on his way to report his suspicions at Bishopsgate police station when he came across Police Constables Ernest Woodhams and Walter Choat on their beat. They agreed to keep watch until Piper could get reinforcements. When he returned there was a total of 7 uniformed policemen – 3 sergeants (Robert Bentley, Bryant and Charles Tucker) and 4 constables (among them Piper, Woodhams and Choat) – and 2 plain-clothes officers.

142

[Plan of the area showing how the burglars hoped to gain access to Samuel's shop in Houndsditch from Exchange Buildings (top). Today the site of Harris' business is a modern office block with a coffee shop on the ground floor (bottom left). Looking at the shop backs from Clothier Street (where Exchange Buildings once stood), with 'The Gherkin' behind. The site of Harris' shop was the building on the right (bottom right)]

143

Bentley went and knocked on the door of No. 11, and the same man came and answered. Bentley asked him to fetch somebody who spoke better English, and while he was gone Bentley made the mistake of entering the hallway (with Bryant and Woodhams just behind). It soon became apparent that they were not alone, and the thing next they knew was the back door opening and gunshots being fired. Bentley received a bullet in the shoulder and another in the neck. He fell back through the doorway. More shots were fired and this time Bryant was hit in the chest and arm. Woodhams and Tucker (who had come to assist) also came under fire, the former receiving a bullet in the thigh, while Tucker was shot in the hip and through the heart.

Charles Tucker, Robert Bentley and Walter Choate all of whom lost their lives in the line of duty on the 16th December 1910 (top from left to right). George Gardstein (bottom left), and Peter the Painter (bottom right)]

Next 3 men and a woman came out of the building as they tried to make their escape. Choat grappled with one of the men (who it later transpired was the gang's leader, George Gardstein) until he received 4 bullets in the leg from Gardstein and 2 in the back from another member of the gang. Gardstein also was also wounded in the crossfire but still managed to get away.

Bentley, Tucker, and Choat all died from their injuries. Gardstein also died from his wound the following morning at No. 59 Grove Street (now Golding Street), the residence of Svaars (and another who went by the name of Peter the Painter). His body was recovered by the police after a doctor, who was not aware of the events of the previous evening, and who had been called to attend Gardstein reported his death to the coroner who in turn informed the police. In fact, when the police arrived at No. 59 a woman by the name of Sara Trassjonsky was in the next room burning papers. She was promptly arrested with the papers seized providing vital information on various groups of anarchists operating in the East End.

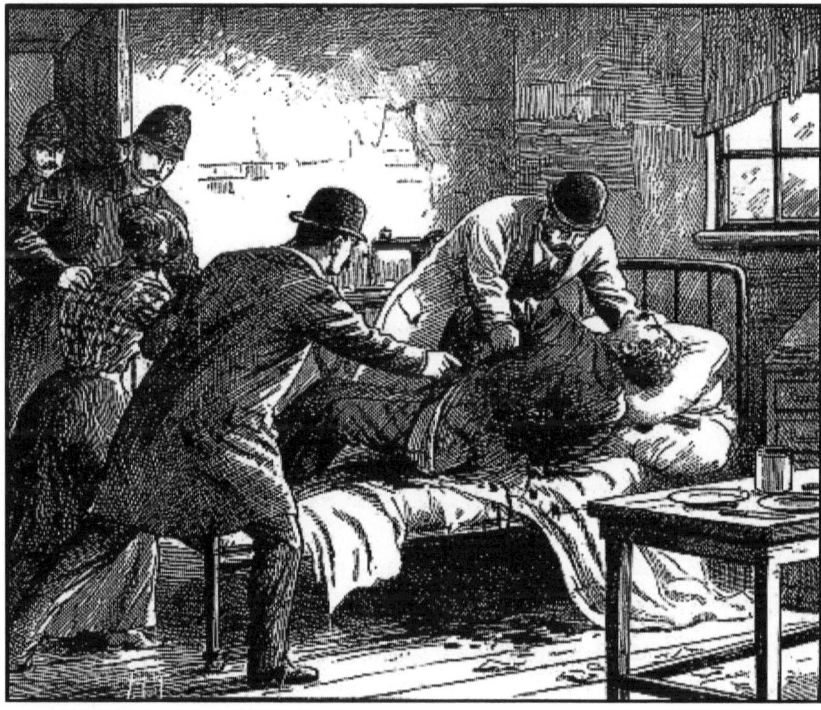

[Police finding Gardstein's body as reported in *The Illustrated Police News*]

Further investigation by around 90 detectives who were seconded to the case, revealed that Gardstein was the leader of a group of Latvian anarchists who went by the name of Leesma (meaning flame). It was thought that in total the anarchists numbered around a dozen followers whose purpose it was to raise funds for Lenin and the Bolshevik movement. By the end of the year several members of Leesma, including Nina Vassilleva, Osip Federoff, Yourka Dubof and Jacob Peters (who it is now thought was not only present at the attempted robbery, but was also the man responsible for killing the 3 police officers), were in police custody. However, there was not to be a conclusion to the case until the Sidney Street Siege the following year (see page 151)

[The memorial service at St. Paul's Cathedral]

On the 22nd December there was a public memorial service for the fallen police officers at St. Paul's Cathedral. In the congregation was Edward Wallington (who represented King George V), the Lord Mayor of London and Winston Churchill (the Home Secretary). Some 10,000 Londoners came to show their respects, shops closed and even the Stock Exchange ceased trading for 30 minutes to allow traders to watch the procession pass along Threadneedle Street. After the service the 3 coffins were transported on an 8 mile journey to various cemeteries, with an estimated 750,000 people lining the route and throwing flowers onto the hearses.

[The memorial plaque unveiled 100 years later in Cutler Street]

Exactly 100 years later on the 16th December 2010 police commissioner Mike Bowron unveiled a plaque to the dead officers on a wall in Cutler Street, behind Houndsditch – the closest location today to where No. 11 Exchange Buildings once stood.

HOUNDSDITCH

[An 1809 drawing and engraving by Augustus Pugin and Thomas Rowlandson of the Great Synagogue at Duke's Place, Houndsditch]

The derivation of the name Houndsditch is unclear. The origin may be found in the fact that the street runs along the site of a former moat/ditch that bounded the City wall where it was reported that there was 'much filth especially dead dogges were laid or cast'. Equally it could refer to the City kennels (which kept hounds for the City hunts) which were located in the moat. Between 1511 and 1571 there was a gun factory in the vicinity, but by the 1590s the ditch had been levelled and houses and carpenters' yards built on the land. Most of the houses were occupied by old-clothes sellers, many of whom died in the great plague and joined the 1,100 or so bodies disposed of in a large nearby ditch. This is a third possible reason for the street name and area.

There remained an old clothes market here right up to the 19th century. For a 1d. fee a prospective customer could gain access to a large room with no stalls, but with sacks of old clothes placed on the floor. By 1861 the area was known for its many Jewish merchants, warehousemen, manufacturers, and inferior jewellery shops.

When Jews were allowed by Cromwell to return to England in 1650, it was at Duke's Place, Houndsditch that German and Polish Jews built the first synagogue in London. It was known as the Great Synagogue, and as the number of worshipers grew so did the synagogue, so that by 1790 there had been 3 versions of the building – each larger and more elegant than the previous. Unfortunately, the synagogue was destroyed by enemy bombing in 1941. Just around the corner is another synagogue at Bevis Marks which, although it was built a decade later, can now claim to be the oldest in the country in continuous use.

CITY OF LONDON POLICE.

MURDER OF POLICE OFFICERS.

£500 REWARD

WHEREAS Sergeants Charles Tucker and Robert Bentley, and Constable Walter Charles Choat, of the City of London Police, were murdered in Exchange Buildings, in the said City, at 11.30 p.m., on the 16th December, 1910, by a man who is now dead, and other persons now wanted, whose descriptions are given below, and who were also concerned with the deceased Murderer in attempting to feloniously break and enter a Jeweller's shop, and killed the Officers to prevent arrest.

PORTRAIT AND DESCRIPTION OF THE DEAD MURDERER.

Name said to be GEORGE GARDSTEIN, alias POOLKA MILOWITZ.

Both may be incorrect.

DESCRIPTION:—

Age about 24, height 5ft. 9 in., complexion pale, hair brown, slight dark moustache worn slightly up at ends, good physique.

DESCRIPTION OF THE PERSONS WANTED.

FIRST.—A man named FRITZ SVARRS, lately residing at 59, Grove Street, Commercial Road, London, E., age about 24 or 25, height 5 feet 8 or 9 inches, complexion sallow, hair fair, medium moustache—turned up at ends, lighter in colour than hair of head—eyes grey, nose rather small—slightly turned up—chin a little upraised, has a few small pimples on face, cheek-bones prominent, shoulders square, but bend slightly forward ; dress brown tweed suit (thin light stripes), dark melton overcoat (velvet collar, nearly new), usually wears a grey Irish tweed cap (red stripes), but has been sometimes seen wearing a trilby hat ; a Locksmith; native of Libau, Russia.

SECOND.—A man known as "PETER THE PAINTER," also lately residing at 59, Grove Street, Commercial Road, London, E., age 28 to 30, height 5 feet 9 or 10 inches, complexion sallow, hair and medium moustache black, clear skin, eyes dark, medium build, reserved manner ; dress brown tweed suit (broad dark stripes), black overcoat (velvet collar, rather old), black hard felt hat, black lace boots, rather shabby, believed to be a native of Russia.

Both are Anarchists.

THIRD.—A woman, age 26 to 30, height 5 feet 4 inches, slim build, fairly full breasts, complexion medium, face somewhat drawn, eyes blue, hair brown ; dress dark three-quarter jacket and skirt, white blouse, large black hat (trimmed black silk), light-coloured shoes.

The above reward of £500 will be paid by the Commissioner of Police for the City of London to any person who shall give such information as shall lead to the arrest of these persons, or in proportion to the number of such persons who are arrested.

Information to be given to the City Police Office, 26, Old Jewry, London, E.C., or at any Police Station.

City Police Office,
26, Old Jewry, London, E.C.
22nd December, 1910.

J. W. NOTT BOWER,
Commissioner of Police for
the City of London.

[City of London wanted poster featuring George Gardstein]

17. THE SIEGE OF SIDNEY STREET
WHITECHAPEL (1911)

The conclusion to the Houndsditch Murders (see page 141) was to take place in
Sidney Street, a non-descript thoroughfare linking Whitechapel Road (see page
77) and Commercial Road. Posters featuring a photograph of George Gardstein
(the leader of the group of Latvian anarchists calling themselves Leesma who had
been responsible for the murders of 3 police officers in the abortive Houndsditch
burglary) and requesting further information were to bear fruit on New Year's
Day 1911, when a member of the public, Charles Perelman, told police that two
of the anarchists, Fritz Svaars and Josef Sokoloff, were hiding on the second floor
at No. 100 Sidney Street. Also there was Sokoloff's mistress, Betty Gershon (who
owned the flat). The informer knew of these people because he had been a
landlord to various members of Leesma. The informer was persuaded to return to
the property the next day just to verify that they were all still there. They were,
and on that basis a meeting took place that afternoon at which various high-
ranking members of the Metropolitan and City police forces were present.

[Armed police take up their positions]

The outcome was that just after midnight some 200 police officers sealed off the
area which was then evacuated house by house. Gershon was also arrested when
a ground floor resident went and fetched her on the pretext that she was needed
by the tenant's sick husband. At 7.30 a.m. the police made their move and knocked
on the door of the anarchists. There was no response so Detective Inspector

151

Frederick Wensley (who was in charge of Whitechapel's CID) threw pebbles up at the windows to wake the two men and inform them of their position. It elicited a response in the form of gunfire with Police Sergeant Ben Leeson being wounded in the lungs and foot. The two anarchists were armed with Mauser pistols, a weapon far superior to anything the police had.

[The Scots Guards take up position in Sidney Street]

152

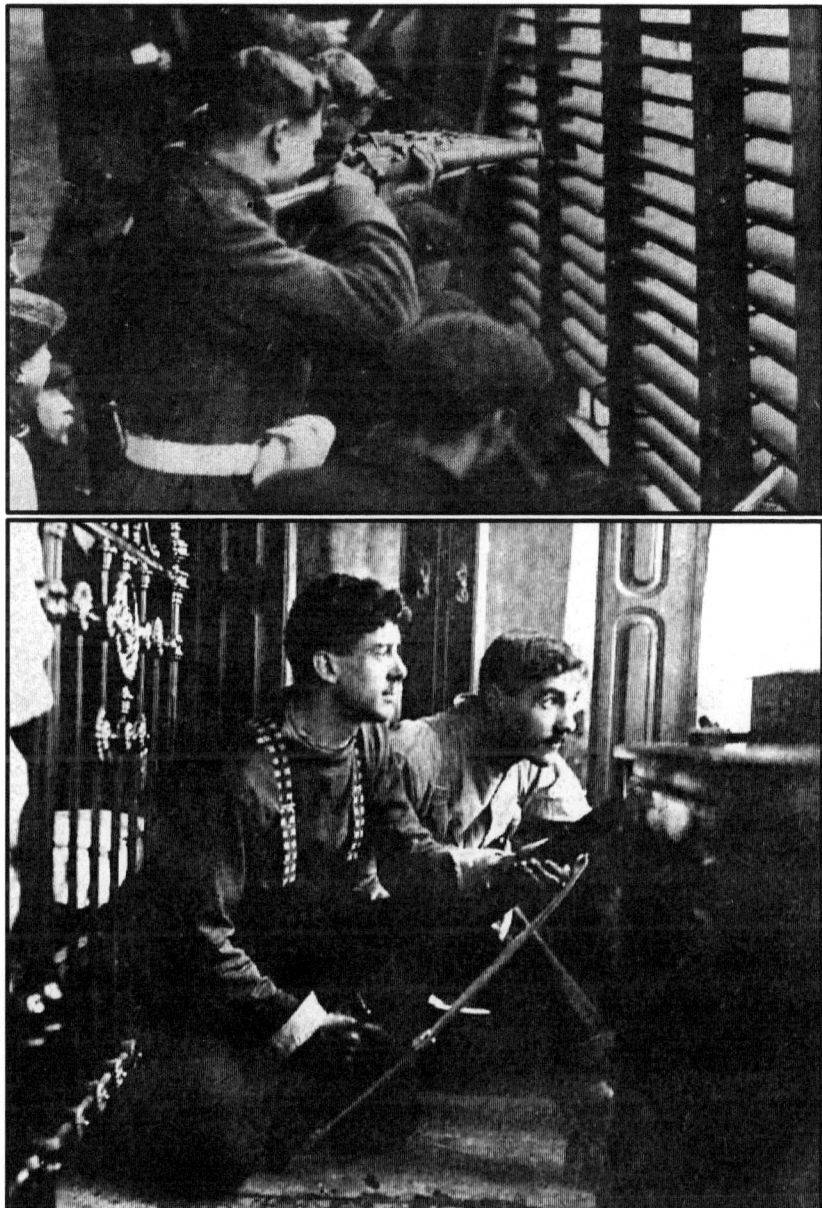

[Not all the Scots Guards were in open positions]

[Winston Churchill, at the scene (top). Reinforcements arrive in the form of more Scots Guards and a Maxim machine gun (bottom)]

154

It was then that Deputy Commissioner Major Frederick Wodehouse at Scotland Yard was contacted, and a request was made for army reinforcements with superior weapons. The Home Secretary's approval was sought and soon 21 marksmen from the Scots Guards stationed at the Tower of London were on their way to Sidney Street. By 10.45 a.m. they were on station, and managed to drive the gunmen to the ground floor. Winston Churchill (who was the Home Secretary at the time) was on the scene himself by midday, and it is thought that this is the only time that a Home Secretary has taken charge of an operational incident (though later Churchill was to say that he was just an observer and made no operational decisions). By now large numbers of the public were gathering so approximately 500 police officers were employed for crowd control. It was thought that heavier firepower was needed so a Maxim machine gun (which was never actually used) was sent for (along with a second detachment of Scots Guards), but around 1 p.m., before its arrival, the house caught fire.

[Royal Horse Artillery arriving with a 13-pounder field gun]

With smoke increasing one of the men put his head out of a window and was promptly shot by a soldier. As the fire took hold, Churchill intervened to ensure that the fire brigade should not risk their lives in trying to extinguish it, only to stop it spreading to neighbouring properties. All gunfire had ceased by 2.30 p.m. and soon after the roof of the building collapsed.

[Churchill with fire officer (top). The fire at takes hold (bottom left). After the roof collapses firemen get to work (bottom right)]

156

It was now clear to all that nobody was still alive inside, so the fireman were allowed enter the building (just as 2 Royal Horse Artillery 13-pounder field guns arrived from St. John's Wood Barracks). On entering the building, the firemen soon found two bodies, one had died from a bullet, and the other from smoke inhalation. Sadly, a wall was to collapse on a group of 5 firemen, with the senior fire officer, Charles Pearson, dying of his injuries some 6 months later. During the day 3 onlookers were also slightly hurt, a reporter's overcoat was ripped by a bullet, and a dog and stray cat were killed in crossfire.

**[Today Wexford House stands on the site of No. 100 Sidney Street (left).
The plaque to Charles Pearson at Wexford House (right)]**

There is a memorial plaque to Charles Pearson at the block of flats called Wexford House that now occupies the site.

A POLICEMAN'S LOT IN 1910

[Directing traffic, and making an arrest for a minor offence were just 2 of the duties undertaken by the early 20th century police constable – murder investigations were thankfully rare]

In 1910 the crime rate was much lower than today. Typically, an officer would be called out to bring order at public house brawls, intervene in quarrels with noisy street traders, and investigate burglaries and robberies. Murder enquiries were very rare   records show that there were just 8 homicide cases a year per million population in England and Wales.

The uniform was much more primitive than that of the 21st century police officer. It consisted of trousers (for both summer and winter), a high collar tunic complete with brass buttons, a winter greatcoat, helmet, cape, belt, boots, and a duty armlet band to be worn on the left sleeve when on duty. As for accessories a policeman would carry a pocket notebook, stout boxwood truncheon, Darby handcuffs (single locking and non-adjustable), and a whistle suspended from a brass chain from the second button of the tunic. A new addition from 1907 was an ambulance call box key.

All police officers had to be at least 5 feet 10 inches tall, with many being over 6 feet tall and recruited from the military. They also had to be of good character, with references commonly being sought from doctors and magistrates, or anybody in a position of authority. In addition, they needed to pass a medical examination.

The wages were in line with other workers at around 26 shillings a week for men, but under half that amount for women. Pay would rise annually by a shilling up to a maximum of 33 shillings for a constable. At the other end of the scale was a superintendent whose salary was £400 per year. The hours of work were either a single, or split shift, of 8 hours a day or night.

However, there were benefits in the form of subsidised accommodation, health care, training, education and a pension. For example, those officers of the City of London police were expected to live in City-owned accommodation, and if married were housed in flats at the rear of Bishopsgate police station (see page 142). If they wished to move elsewhere, they would need permission to do so from the Commander. Additionally, the City of London police had accommodation blocks in the East End and Brixton (south of the Thames). These section houses for single men were a sort of police barracks, but roomy, well-appointed, and homely. For the cost of around 7 shillings a week the officer could expect a comfortable bed, a hot dinner daily, and the use of the common rooms. The provision of free health care was a big bonus, as was the receiving of a pension – though this was not guaranteed as it was dependent upon a good conduct record. The pension was paid at a rate of $^2/_3{}^{rd}$ the officer's salary after 26 years of service.

The training element included being taught self-defence, how to march, salute, patrol, and administer first-aid. Education included officers having to take exams in reading, writing, maths, and philosophy.

In conclusion a policeman's lot at this time was an arduous one, but one with excellent benefits, most prized of which was the pension which made a fitting conclusion to the career of the long-suffering guardian of the London public.

18. The Murder of Solomon Millstein Liverpool Street (1912)

[Coverage of the Millstein murder in *The Illustrated Police News*]

Hanbury Street is synonymous with the murder of Annie Chapman by Jack the Ripper at No. 29 (see page 98), but No. 62 was to become a double crime scene some 24 years later. The premises was a simple eating house owned by a Russian Jew called Solomon Millstein and his wife Annie who had been in business here for around 20 years. While to any passerby the restaurant looked respectable enough, the basement doubled as an illegal gambling den (for which Millstein was paying protection money to the local police).

[Today No. 62 Hanbury Street is a Japanese restaurant]

In the early morning of the 27th December 1912 the building caught fire. Marks Verbloot, a tenant on the top floor had smelt smoke, opened his window, and raised the alarm by blowing a police whistle. Firemen acted promptly and on entering the first-floor back bedroom found a burning bed which they extinguished. Beside the bed was the body of Annie in a pool of blood. She had been hit over the head with a poker, stabbed, and strangled. Close by was Solomon, who had also been knocked down and stabbed to death with a large kitchen knife. The time of death was estimated to be around 3.30 a.m. Money from the restaurant was missing but nothing else it seemed.

The murderer was careless and as he left behind both his footprints, where he had stepped in the pool of blood, and also his bloodstained scarf. The police were soon able to trace the owner of the scarf to a fish porter named Myer (Meyer in some references) Abramovitch. When arrested he was wearing one of Millstein's suits over his own bloodstained clothes, and in addition he had several cuts to his hands. When he was searched, Solomon's watch and chain were found on his person. In his statement to the police, he said that he had lost all his money gambling in the basement on Boxing Day. As a consequence, he had decided to rob the restaurant, but the Millsteins had caught him and in the ensuing fight he had killed them both and started the fire to cover his tracks (similar to the Brick Lane murder – see page 167).

He was put on trial at the Central Criminal Court on the 30th January 1912 and pleaded insanity. However, the prison doctors considered him perfectly sane, and so with the overwhelming evidence against him he was found guilty by the jury after a deliberation of only 10 minutes. He was hanged at Pentonville Prison on the 8th March 1912.

HANBURY STREET

[Hanbury Hall (top left), and the house in which the entertainer Bud Flanagan was born (top right). The tiles embedded in the wall of Hanbury Hall are a reminder of Huguenot influence here (bottom)]

Formerly Browne's Lane (being originally named after the developer of the area in the 17th century), Hanbury Street runs off Commercial Street, across Brick Lane, to the junction with Old Montague Street and Vallance Road in Spitalfields. It was from a small house here in 1884 that Florence Soper, the daughter-in-law of William Booth (founder of The Salvation Army), ran the newly inaugurated Women's Social Work. It was both a safe haven for prostitutes, and a place where it was hoped they would be able to turn away from that trade. The south side of the street (between Commercial Street and Brick Lane) with its flats above and shops below has changed little since Victorian times, though the north side was demolished to make way for the extension of the Old Truman Brewery. The brewery closed in 1989 and today the site of an arts and event centre.

The most notable building in the street is Hanbury Hall which has tiles embedded in the wall which are a reminder of the former Huguenot influence in the area. It was built in 1719 as a small French Huguenot chapel, but over the years it became La Patente Church (1740), a German Lutheran Church (1787), and a United Free Methodists Church prior to becoming part of the Anglican Christ Church in 1887. Charles Dickens was no stranger to the building, using it for public readings of his works, and in 1888 it was here that the 'match girls' held their strike meetings as they began their protest for better working conditions at the nearby Bryant and May factory in Bow. The entertainer Bud Flanagan was born at No. 12 Hanbury Street in 1896.

19. The Murder of Frances Tucker
Aldgate East (1960)

[It was in the 1st floor flat that Frances Tucker's was found strangled]

The victim, Frances Tucker, was a well-known character, both to the residents and the police, in the Brick Lane area during the 1950s. She was a hunchback with

Scottish and West Indian roots who dealt in recreational drugs – mainly West Indian 'reefers' and hemp. Her infirmity did not stop her libido and in early 1960 her boyfriend was unemployed decorator Cleveland Reid who hailed originally from Jamaica.

On the evening of the 11th January 1960 smoke was seen coming through the window of her first floor flat at No. 106 Brick Lane. The fire brigade was called and the 20 occupants of the house were rescued, including several from the roof via a long ladder. Frances Tucker was the only casualty.

However, upon investigation it was soon discovered that she had been strangled prior to paraffin being poured on the floor and ignited in an attempt to conceal the murder. Reid was the obvious suspect, especially so since he had previously made threats against Frances including at one point saying that he would roast her on a Christmas tree with a can of oil. He also had convictions for theft, assault and unlawful wounding, and had only just been released from prison. Their most recent fight had been due to Frances allegedly selling off some of Cleveland's things while he had been away.

Reid was soon tracked down by the police to his sister's house in Cricklewood. When arrested his clothes still smelt of paraffin. In his defence he said that Frances was blackmailing him over a compromising photograph. This led to an argument and him strangling her and setting the house on fire to cover his tracks (in a similar manner to the Millstein case – see page 161). He was tried at the Old Bailey on the 17th March 1960, found guilty, and given a life sentence. At that time there was still the option of hanging

BRICK LANE

[Brick Lane in the early 20th century – always a busy street]

Brick Lane takes its name from the fact that bricks and tiles were manufactured near here from the 16th century. By the middle of the 17th century houses began to appear at the southern end of the lane and a few years later, around 1666, a brewery was located here. The Black Eagle Brewery (better known as Truman's Brewery) was producing 400,000 barrels of beer annually in 1853 (making it the largest in the world). After the partition of Bengal and Union with Pakistan in 1947 the area became home to many thousands of Bengalis.

Today the shops and many restaurants are almost all Bangladeshi. There is also a Saturday market which has its origins in the 18th century when it was a place farmers could sell their livestock and produce outside the City of London boundary, but today it is a place for everything from leather goods, jewellery, and kitchenware to books, plants, and bric-a-brac.

20. The Kray Twins
Whitechapel/Bethnal Green (1966/1967)

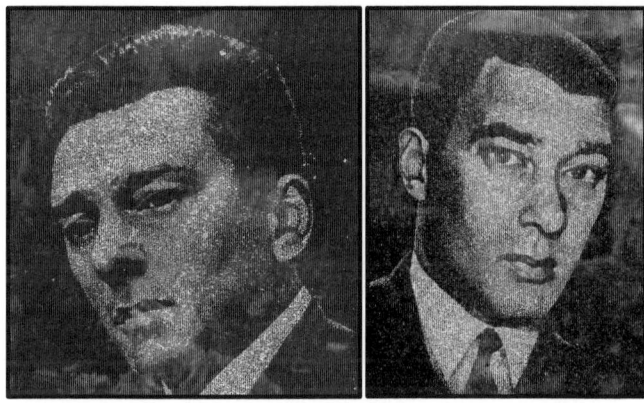

[The Kray twins – Ronnie (left) and Reggie (right)]

The Kray name is instantly recognisable and will ever be associated with the East End in general, and the Blind Beggar public house (see page 176) in particular. The twins, Ronnie and Reggie, were born on the 24th October 1933 and by trade were professional boxers. They may have been smartly dressed and looked respectable, but they were vicious thugs who were to hold a vice-like grip over the East End in the 1950s and for most of the 1960s as well. For example, one man who told Ronnie that he was putting on a few pounds in weight subsequently needed 70 stitches – Ronnie often used his razor to slash people just for the fun of it.

[Site of The Regal billiard hall is now a care home]

Their first Old Bailey appearance was in 1950 under a charge of assault, but due to lack of evidence the case was dismissed. They did National Service in 1952, which saw the twins in trouble with the military authorities for violence with spells spent in custody, and culminating in dishonourable discharges. After that they could no longer box professionally so became nightclub bouncers, before moving up a league into the protection racket business. Their first enterprise was a rundown billiard hall called The Regal in Eric Street, Mile End (long since demolished and rebuilt as a care home). They also worked for another villain, Jay Murray, through whom they became involved with hijacking, armed robbery and arson. It was a lucrative time and gave them the capital with which to start their empire.

[Long Grove, near Epsom in Surrey]

Their next run in with the law was on the 5th November 1956 when Ronnie led an attack on a man called Terence Martin who received a bayonet wound from one of the gang members. Ronnie was sentenced to 3 years imprisonment, but spent much of the time at Long Grove, a mental hospital near Epsom in Surrey, having been diagnosed with paranoid schizophrenia. It became clear at this time that Ronnie was a homosexual (though he claimed that he was bisexual) and had a strong dislike of women. Actually, both men were to marry twice (Ronnie to Elaine Mildener in 1985 and Kate Howard in 1989; Reggie to Frances Shea in 1965 – who committed suicide in 1967 – and Roberta Jones in 1997).

In February 1960 it was Reggie's turn to be imprisoned for 18 months for protection-related threats. Ironically it was while he was in prison that Ronnie got control of Esmeralda's Barn nightclub in Knightsbridge via Peter Rachman, the head of a violent landlord operation. It cost just £1,000 despite having a turnover of £500,000 per year – the twins got personal incomes of £40,000 each per year from this venture. The twins were helped in their business activities by Alan Cooper – he was a banker who needed the Krays' protection from the rival Richardson gang in South London.

Their legitimate enterprises thrived and soon they were the owners of various restaurants and nightclubs. The establishments were frequented by both show business stars of the day and politicians. The police investigated the activities of the Krays on several occasions but their reputation for violence resulted, quite understandably, in nobody coming forward to volunteer information.

The shooting on the 9th March 1966 at the Blind Beggar public house in Whitechapel Road was to change everything and see the tide turn against the Krays. George Cornell had grown up with the twins and been a friend, but now worked for the Richardsons. The previous Christmas at a meeting of the Krays and Richardsons at the Astor Club, Cornell had referred to Ronnie as a 'fat poof' – something Ronnie was unlikely to forget in a hurry. The day before the Blind Beggar incident, Richard Hart, a member of the 'The Firm' as the Krays called their gang, had been killed in a shootout at Mr. Smith's Club in Catford, after which most of the Richardsons' gang had been arrested. Cornell had escaped arrest, and on the 9th March had been at The Royal London Hospital in Whitechapel visiting his wounded gang members, and afterwards simply chose the Blind Beggar as a public house in the vicinity in which to have a quiet drink before (presumably) returning to South London. When this news reached Ronnie, who was himself in a public house (The Lion in Tapp Street) under a mile away, he was infuriated and along with John Dickson (his driver) and Ian Barrie he decided to teach Cornell a lesson, and also get revenge for Hart. At 8.30 p.m. Ronnie and Barrie entered the Blind Beggar with Barrie firing shots into the ceiling to act as a warning. Cornell, who was sitting at the bar, remarked, 'well just look who's here' moments before Ronnie shot him through the eye. Ironically, playing on the jukebox was the current hit by the Walker Brothers, *The Sun Ain't Gonna Shine Anymore*. Strangely not a single person in the public house saw a thing, even the barmaid was busy in the cellar changing pumps. Reggie was later to comment on the incident saying that 'Ronnie does some funny things'.

In December 1966 the Krays were responsible for helping Frank 'Mad Axeman' Mitchell escape from Dartmoor Prison. However, with a police manhunt in progress and Mitchell becoming increasingly unstable and violent while on the run, the twins had him killed off with the body being dumped in the English Channel.

Having committed murder, it was Ronnie's turn to goad Reggie. So to even the score Reggie was tasked with disposing of Jack 'the hat' McVitie (so called as he always wore a hat to cover his baldness) who had also made satirical remarks about the brothers. Ronnie had given a gun and £100 to McVitie with orders to kill their financial adviser, Leslie Payne. This was to have been followed by another £400 upon completion of the job. Reggie subsequently went to get the £100 back (as the job had not been done), but was so moved by McVitie's explanation that he ended up giving him £50. Ronnie was not so impressed, and had McVitie invited to a party in Evering Road, Stoke Newington on the 29th October 1967. The intention was to shoot him with a Mauser, but the gun jammed twice so it was left to Reggie to stab him to death. How many times it is not known since the body was never found, but Reggie did tell Ronnie that 'you want to try it sometime it's a nice feeling'.

[The house in Evering Road where Jack 'the hat' McVitie was murdered]

The Chicago-style antics of the brothers was becoming too much for the Metropolitan Police so a squad was formed under Detective Superintendent Leonard 'Nipper' Read to smash their empire of crime. Having diligently collected sufficient evidence for convictions on multiple crimes, at dawn on the 8th May 1968 some 68 officers made raids all over the East End. The twins were arrested and went to trial with crucial testimony coming from the barmaid at the Blind Beggar (who was now willing to give evidence having been given a new identity), and other gang members who had been offered attractive deals. After a 40 day trial 10 of the gang members received prison sentences, with the twins being sent down for life with a non-parole period of 30 years each. As Justice Melford Stevenson put it 'in my view, society has earned a rest from you're your activities'. Ronnie died in Broadmoor (a mental institution) in 1995, while Reggie was only released in August 2000 when it was revealed that he was in the end stages of bladder cancer from which he died a few weeks later.

[The Krays' family plot at Chingford Mount Cemetery, with the most dominant memorial belonging to Frances Kray, who committed suicide just 2 years after her marriage to Reggie Kray]

Both funerals attracted thousands who lined the streets to applaud as the cortege went past. Many were no doubt relieved, while others showed genuine signs of sorrow since their gangland activities had protected the East End from social crimes such as child abuse and rape. The twins commanded both fear and admiration from locals. They were buried together in Chingford Mount Cemetery.

It should be noted that the Krays had an elder brother, Charles Kray, who was also a member of 'The Firm' and who spent much of his life in prison. He was released after 10 years in 1975, but was later convicted of drug offences in 1997 and died in prison 3 years later.

Although this is probably the most recent East End case that will be familiar to the reader, the problem of gangs in London has not gone away. The emphasis has changed though with there being a heavier involvement with the sale and distribution of drugs, often using young teenagers who are tempted by what they perceive as the prospect of easy money, respect, and power. The Metropolitan Police set up Operation Trident in 1998 to deal with murders perpetrated by black gangsters against other black persons, but it is now a permanent squad dealing with all aspects of gangs and gun crime.

For the 'location detective' it is fortunate that the story of the Krays is relatively modern so many of the places associated with them still exist.

THE BLIND BEGGAR PUBLIC HOUSE

[The Blind Beggar]

In 1894 the Blind Beggar public house was built on the site of an inn that had been established before 1654. In fact, it was adjacent to the Manns Albion brewery, responsible for the first modern Brown Ale, and served as its brewery tap i.e. the nearest outlet to a brewery which by default is thought to serve the 'freshest' beer. In fact, it was the landlord of the public house who in 1808 bought the brewery next door. The name of the public house is taken from the legend of Henry de Montfort, who was wounded and lost his sight at the Battle of Evesham in 1265.

He survived thanks to a baroness who nursed him back to health, and who was later to have a child named Besse with him. He became known as the 'Blind Beggar of Bethnal Green' and used to beg at the crossroads where the public house now stands. It was close to here that William Booth, the founder of the Salvation Army, preached his first sermon. On not such a charitable note it is also where Ronnie Kray murdered George Cornell in the bar on the 9th March 1966 (see page 176).

THE CARPENTERS ARMS PUBLIC HOUSE

The Krays were brought up mainly by their mother, Violet, since their father, Charles, was often away on business travelling the country as a furniture dealer. Clearly the boys loved their mother so it is no surprise that in 1967 they bought her the mid-Victorian Carpenters Arms at No. 73 Cheshire Street (on the corner of St. Matthew's Row and backing onto the Krays' former primary school – see page 187), and decorated it in a Regency style to match their nightclub (Esmeralda's Barn) in the West End. Apart from hanging their boxing gloves over the bar it has become legend/myth that the bar counter was comprised of coffin lids.

[The Carpenters Arms]

Prior to their ownership of the place they had frequently held meetings of 'The Firm' here throughout the 1960s, and it was from here that they set off to Stoke Newington on the night that Jack 'the hat' McVitie was murdered by Reggie (see page 174). The pub held happy memories for the Krays as it was also the place where they would hold Christmas and New Year parties. Inside there are still reminders of the past in the form of a modern portrait of the twins and various weapons (hammers, pliers, bats, and knives) displayed in a cabinet in the back room.

W. ENGLISH & SON FUNERAL DIRECTORS

[The 'undertakers to the underworld']

The family firm of W. English & Son have been conducting funerals for over 200 years. It was from their premises, in Bethnal Green Road, that they arranged the funerals of Ronnie Kray (1995), Reggie Kray (2000), and Charlie Kray (2000), and thus became known locally as 'undertakers of the underworld'. For Reggie's funeral this involved the provision of an old-fashioned glass hearse pulled by 6 black horses, the contours of their black harnesses and blinkers picked-out with silver lines, and 18 inch tall black plumes rising from the top of their heads.

On the left side of the hearse was a wreath of white and red flowers which spelt out 'free at last', while on the roof was another of just white flowers with the single word 'respect'. It was very much a media event with television vans, photographers, and even a helicopter present. There were many curious onlookers in groups, although not as many as for Ronnie Kray's funeral when the streets were lined with people the entire length of the route from the funeral directors to St. Matthew's Church (see page 184). Security was provided by former gang members in black overcoats with red armbands. After the service the coffin was taken by motorised hearse to the family plot at Chingford Mount Cemetery where there was a flypast by a Spitfire hired from Duxford air museum.

THE GRAVE MAURICE PUBLIC HOUSE

The Grave Maurice is an ex-public house dating from 1874 located at No. 269 Whitechapel Road, and was a favourite haunt of Ronnie Kray. The unusual name is derived from Maurits van Nassau, the Prince of Orange, who led a revolt against the Spanish in the 16th century.

Upstairs there was a full-size snooker table (unused for 40 years) and a valuable Elizabethan blanket box in which logs for the open fire were kept. Most famously Ronnie Kray gave a press interview here with detective Superintendent Read, who went out of curiosity, in the audience out of curiosity. Being so close to The Royal London Hospital it was always popular with doctors and other hospital workers, but trade declined such that it closed in 2010 and since then the premises has been split into two businesses – a betting shop and a pawnbrokers.

[The name of the former public house, built in 1874, is still visible in the stonework]

THE LION PUBLIC HOUSE

[Now flats, the architecture is that of a typical Victorian public house (left)]

No longer a public house, the building was converted some years ago into flats. This was where, on the 9th March 1966, Ronnie Kray was drinking when he learnt that George Cornell was close by having a drink at the Blind Beggar public house (see page 176).

MULBERRY ACADEMY SHOREDITCH

The academy school, which now stands in Gossett Street, has gone through several name changes, but in the 1940s was Daniel Street School (founded in 1900) where the Krays underwent their secondary education between 1944 and 1949. It was here that they first got into scraps, and also while here that they started boxing.

[The Kray's secondary school]

PELLICCI'S CAFÉ

[Still a favourite for good food at reasonable prices]

180

A favourite haunt of the Krays and other members of 'The Firm' was Pellicci's Café at No. 332 Bethnal Green Road. Places where you could get home-cooked food at a reasonable price were once common in London (numbering around 2,000 at their peak in the inter-war years) but are now an endangered species. Priamo Pellicci started his business in 1900, and it was here that he and his wife, Elide, brought up their 7 children. It has been in the family ever since and today it is run by Maria Pellicci who has been cooking here since 1966. The building is Grade II listed thanks in no small measure to the ornate marquetry panelled wooden décor which was carved by Achille Capocci in 1946.

REPTON BOXING CLUB & PUBLIC BATHS

[The building in which the Kray twins learnt their trade]

It was at Repton Boxing Club that the Krays learned to box in their youth. They made the finals of the London Boxing Championships on 3 occasions. Their peak was in 1951 when they both appeared in a middleweight contest at the Royal Albert Hall. In total Ronnie fought 6 professional fights, 4 of which he won, while Reggie was more successful winning all 6 of his. It was just outside this club that, in January 1965, member of 'The Firm' Freddie 'Brown Bread' (nothing to do with his eating habits!) Foreman, an armed robber and also the man who helped

181

dispose of Jack 'The Hat' McVitie's body (see page 174), shot Ginger Marks dead in retaliation for him having shot his brother in the legs. Foreman was also responsible for killing Frank 'Mad Axeman' Mitchell (see page 173).

[The ring where *non viscara … non gloria* (no guts … no glory) is the motto]

The boxing club, which is located in Cheshire Street, is London's oldest boxing gym and was founded by Repton College (an independent fee-paying boarding school in Derbyshire) in 1884 (as Repton Boys Club) as a place where underprivileged boys could go to get out of crime in the area. The sponsorship continued until 1971. Today it has a reputation as the strongest boxing club in the country and has been responsible for over 500 champions including John H. Stracey, Maurice Hope, Olympians such as Micky Carter, Billy Taylor, Dave Odwell, Graham Moughton, Gary Barker, Sylvester Mitte, Audley Harrison, and Tony Cesay. Adjacent to it is the bath house, which the Krays would have used on a frequent basis. The public baths and wash houses provided hot water and laundry facilities, as well as a hot bath (and a clean towel) thus making it an essential part of East London life in an area where so many homes, such as the Krays' own home in Vallance Road (see page 186), had no bathroom. The baths are long gone having been converted into flats, though the façade remains.

[The bath house would have been well-known to the Kray twins]

ST. JAMES THE GREAT CHURCH

['The Red' church is now residential flats]

Known locally as 'The Red' church due to its red brickwork this is where on the 19th April 1965 Reggie married Frances Shea in what at the time could have been mistaken for a Society wedding given the number of high-profile guests. A young David Bailey was the wedding photographer – his first such commission. Shea would be returning to the church 2 years later for her funeral following her suicide. She is buried in the Kray's family plot in Chingford Mount Cemetery (see page 175).

183

The church was built in 1844 in an Early English style by Edward Blore (who had previously worked on Buckingham Palace, Lambeth Palace, Westminster Abbey, and St. James' Palace). It was very much a commercial enterprise from the start as the first vicar, Edward Coke, offered marriages in batches for only 7d., though later he was to make it the first church in London where poor couples could marry for free. Coke was most enterprising for he also raised funds for a dispensary, a visiting society, and a Sunday School. The building survived World War II intact, but falling numbers of churchgoers meant that it was closed in 1987, and today has been converted to residential use.

St. Matthew's Church

[The church where the funeral services for all 3 Kray brothers took place]

St. Matthew's Church in St. Matthews Row played its part in the story of the Krays for it was here that the funeral services for all three brothers (Charles, Ronnie, and Reggie), and their mother Violet, were held. The history of the church

184

really begins on the 13th October 1725 when the land on which the church stands, Hare Fields, was purchased for £200. However, due to disputes as to the size and design of the building it was not until 1743 that the foundation stone was laid by Ebenezer Mussell. It took 3 years to complete and in 1859 disaster struck when fire destroyed the interior. It was rebuilt in 1861 with a cupola on the tower, iron sanctuary gates, rood figures, stained glass, ornate mural decorations, and a huge stone reredos.

[The interior of St. Matthews Church which dates from the 1960s]

Disaster struck again in 1940 when German bombing left the place as a roofless shell. A temporary structure came into existence in the early 1950s, but in 1957 Antony Lewis was appointed architect and tasked with rebuilding the church as it stands today. The temporary church was demolished in 1960 and the present building re-consecrated on the 15th July 1961. The latest incarnation saw the use of young artists so that the decoration includes Stations of the Cross by Don Potter, a staircase sculpture by Kim James, the Apostles Screen by Peter Snow, and an altar by Robert Dawson. The church also incorporates items, such as some of the stained glass, from other bombed out and disused churches in the area.

VALLANCE ROAD

[The site of 'Fort Vallance' at No. 178 Vallance Road]

In 1938 when the Kray twins were 5-years old their parents moved from No. 64 Stean Street to No. 178 Vallance Road. It was a small terrace house with no bathroom and a toilet in the garden (as was normal in those times). It is here that the twins grew up, and here that they had their headquarters, which they called 'Fort Vallance' – an accurate name considering that there was an armoury under the floorboards and a grinder out back for Ronnie to sharpen his bayonets and swords. The terrace was demolished and replaced by a modern development as part of the self-building housing initiative. There is a plaque outside the current No. 178 that was unveiled by Prince Charles in September 1988.

WILLIAM DAVIS PRIMARY SCHOOL

Formerly the Wood Close School this was the place where the Krays received their primary education until the age of 11 when they went on to the Daniel Street School (see page 180). By all accounts the twins were no more trouble than any other pupil. The school (in Wood Close, Cheshire Street) was built in 1900 as a Board School i.e. under the Elementary Education Act of 1870 local boroughs and parishes could run a school free from Anglican doctrines and administered via a board of elected members.

[The Kray's primary school]

Wood Close School must have been one of the last to be built since Board Schools were abolished by the Education Act of 1902 which replaced them with local educational authorities.

BETHNAL GREEN

[Kirby's Castle, home to the 'blind beggar', circa 1880]

Once considered a pleasant country area, by the Victorian period Bethnal Green had become the poorest district of London. The name is thought to be Saxon and means Blida's corner. The centre of all English villages is the green, and it was here Sir William Ryder, the Deputy Master of Trinity House, built a large mansion called Kirby's Castle in 1570 – it later became the Bethnal House Lunatic Asylum. By 1743 there were about 15,000 people living in 1,800 houses. Many were occupied by those involved with silk-weaving who had moved out of Spitalfields, which had become too expensive. By 1840 a survey estimated that there were 6 times as many looms in Bethnal Green as Spitalfields, however, the survey coincided with a terminal decline of that trade so that by the time Charles Booth made his poverty map of London in 1889 he found that 45% of the population were living below the subsistence level.

It was not all desolate though. In the 1840s the Crown purchased land that became Victoria Park, and in 1872 the Victoria and Albert Museum opened the Museum of Childhood in Cambridge Heath Road, while in Derbyshire Street a university settlement called Oxford House was established in 1884. More recently the slums have been replaced by large council estates, although in an attempt to retain something of the former village atmosphere, Bethnal Green Gardens has been turned into a conservation area. The population has continued to fall in tandem with the further decline of industrial businesses in the district.

MAPS

The following maps show the relative locations of the various places covered in this guide. The table gives information about the closest railway station, other nearby places of interest, and the exact location according to What3Words. It should be noted that many of the sites are set in non-tourist areas of London with a higher than average crime rate – please take this into consideration when planning your visit.

Table of Locations

No.	Place	Station	Page	Map	Near	What 3 Words
1	The Hanging of a Hangman	Old Street	9	5	10	shot. called. shift
2	Dick Turpin Shoots Tom King	Aldgate East	15	2	6/11/ 12/16	saving. pencil. necks
3	The Murder of Venables and Rogers	Stepney Green	21	8	–	senses. pouch. feeds
4	The Ratcliffe Highway Murders	Shadwell/ Wapping	25	9	–	exam. storms. fell
5	The Murder of Carlo Ferrari by 'Burkers'	Shoreditch High Street	37	7	20	economies. belly. acid
6	Eliza Ross: The Last 'Burker'	Tower Gateway/ Tower Hill	47	2	2/12/ 16	funded. level. code
7	The Case of Thomas Briggs' Hat	Hackney Wick	53	4	–	open. clean. select
8	The Artillery Passage Murder	Liverpool Street	65	1	12/16/ 18/19	answer. oils. resort
9	The Murder of Harriet Lane	Whitechapel	71	6	12/14/ 15/17/ 20	stared. rock. cars

189

No.	Place	Station	Page	Map	Near	What 3 Words
10	The Murder of Lydia Green	Old Street	79	5	1	gives. lend. scrap
11	The Batty Street Murder	Aldgate East	87	2	2/12	short. long. appear
12	The Canonical Five Jack the Ripper Murders		95	10		
	Mary Ann 'Polly' Nichols	Whitechapel	95	10	9/14/ 15/17/ 20	jolly. orange. monks
	Annie Chapman	Liverpool Street	98	10	18/19	shell. ahead. doing
	Elizabeth Stride	Aldgate East	105	10	2/11	enter. quest. tinsel
	Catherine Eddowes	Aldgate	109	10	2/6/16	bucket. leap. object
	Mary Kelly	Liverpool Street	115	10	8	kicked. same. taking
13	A Double Killing in Amhurst Road	Hackney Central	123	3	–	span. swaps. cowboy
14	The Double Murder in Turner Street	Whitechapel	129	6	9/12/ 15/17/ 20	undulation. follow. filer
15	Murder at the Lord Nelson public house	Whitechapel	135	6	9/12/ 14/17/ 20	pump. thick. dared

190

No.	Place	Station	Page	Map	Near	What 3 Words
16	The Houndsditch Murders	Liverpool Street/ Aldgate	141	1	2/6/8/ 12	jeeps. thick. casual
17	The Siege of Sidney Street	Whitechapel	151	6	9/12/ 14/15/ 20	petty. prom. cloth
18	The Murder of Solomon Millstein	Liverpool Street	161	1	8/12/ 19	drama. tape. dawn
19	The Murder of Frances Tucker	Liverpool Street	167	1	8/12/ 18	rods. react. perky
20	The Kray Twins		171		-	
	The Blind Beggar public house	Whitechapel	176		9/12/ 14/15/ 17	pushes. lists. notice
	The Carpenters Arms public house	Bethnal Green Mainline	177		-	guides. jolly. silk
	W. English & Son Funeral Directors	Bethnal Green	178		-	hurray. unable. potato
	The Grave Maurice public house	Whitechapel	178		9/12/ 14/15/ 17	lands. wants. much
	The Lion public house	Bethnal Green Mainline	179		-	belts. certified. woes
	Mulberry Academy Shoreditch	Bethnal Green Mainline	180		5	backed. gifted half

No.	Place	Station	Page	Map	Near	What 3 Words
20	Pellicci's Café	Bethnal Green	180		-	things. spaces. trials
	Repton Boxing Club & Public Baths	Bethnal Green Mainline	181		-	rotate. plays. boom
	St. James the Great Church	Bethnal Green	183		-	villa. bond. gossip
	St. Matthew's Church	Bethnal Green Mainline	184		-	trunk. homes. sushi
	Vallance Road	Bethnal Green Mainline	186		-	inform. shift. plays
	William Davis Primary School	Bethnal Green Mainline	187		-	piles. linen. ends

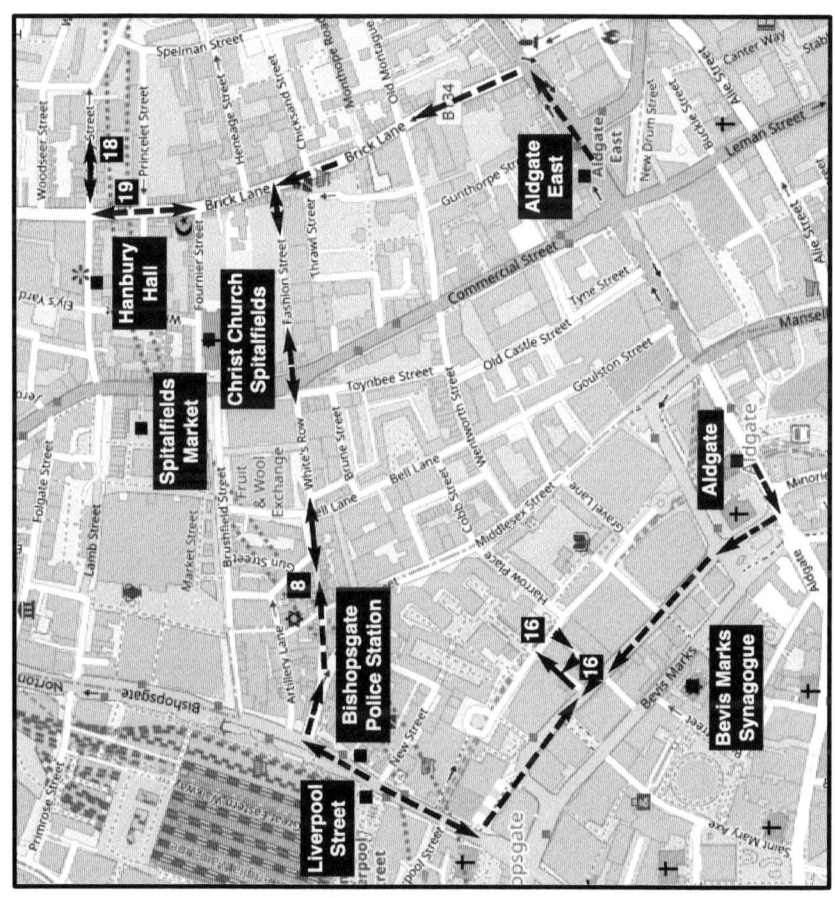

Map 1 – Aldgate, Aldgate East & Liverpool Street

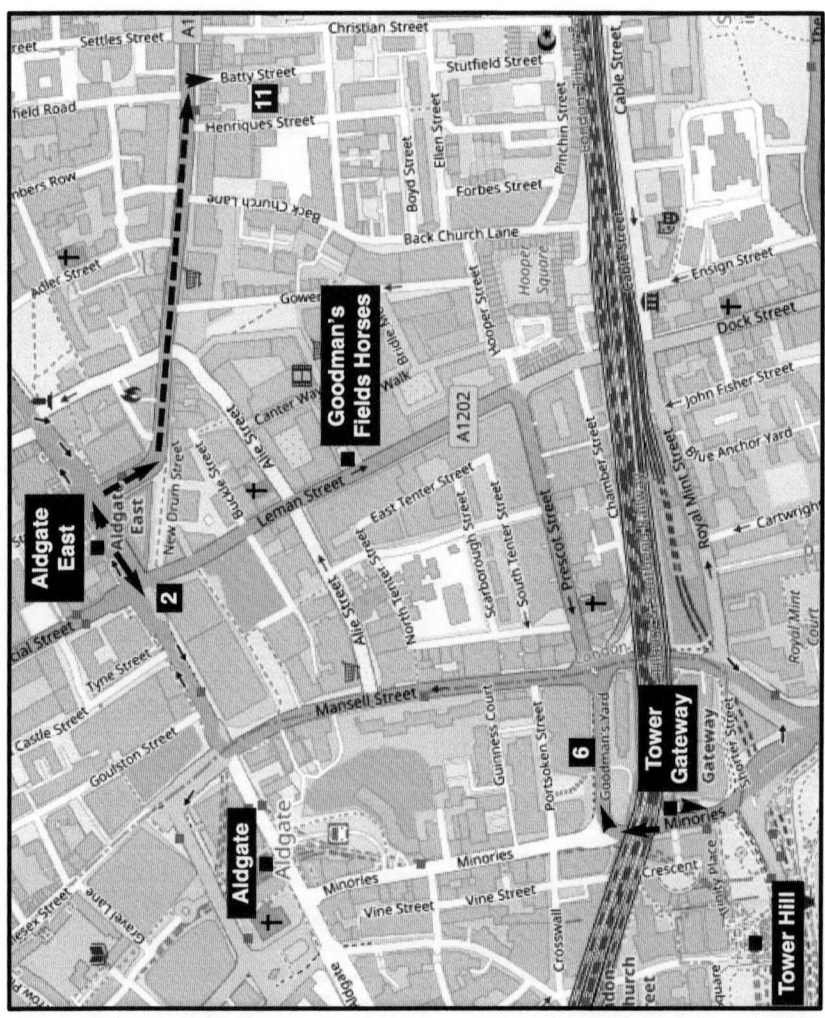

Map 2 – Aldgate, Aldgate East, Tower Gateway & Tower Hill

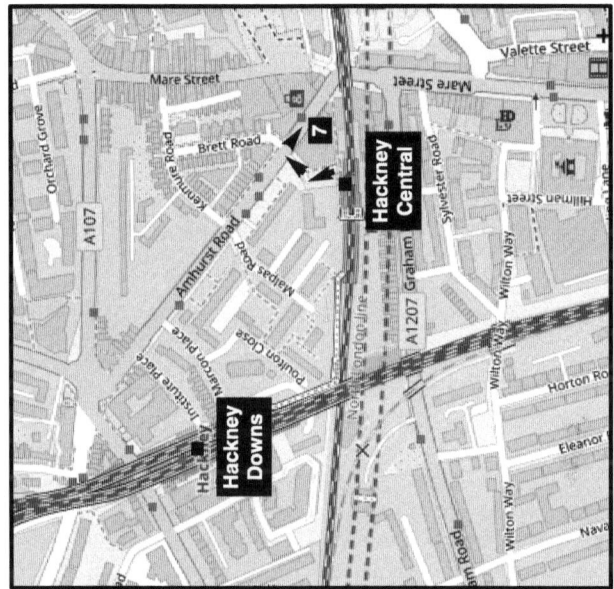

Map 3 – Hackney Central & Hackney Downs

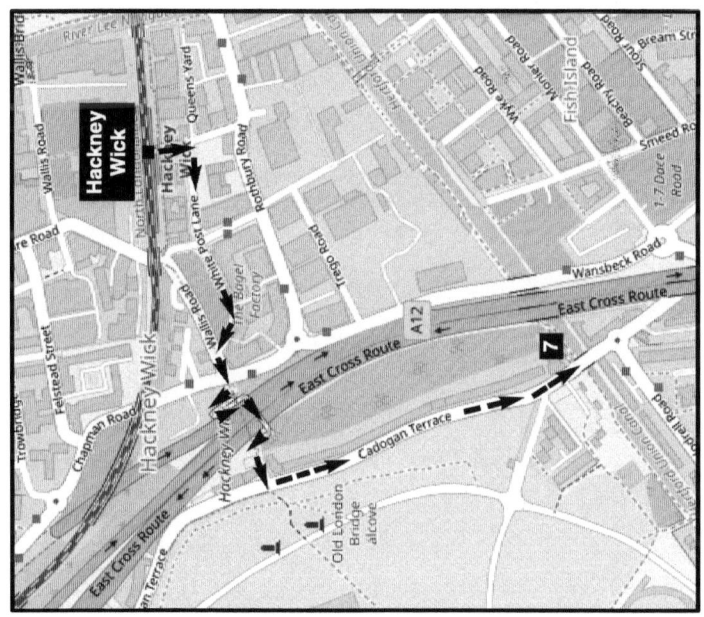

Map 4 – Hackney Wick

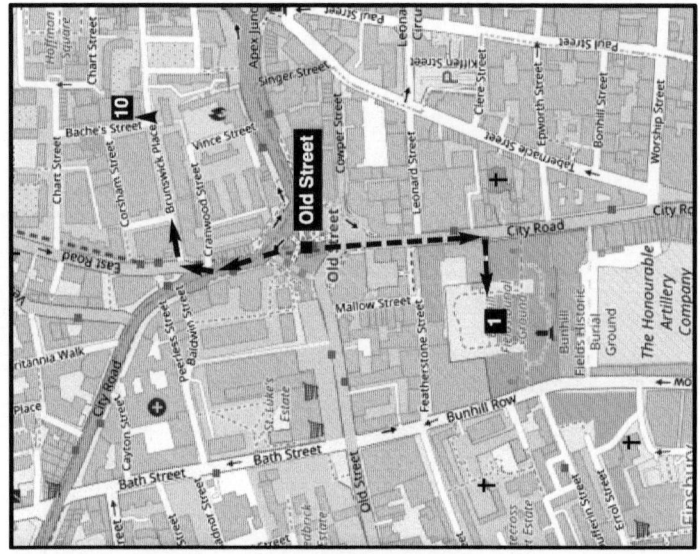

Map 5 – Old Street

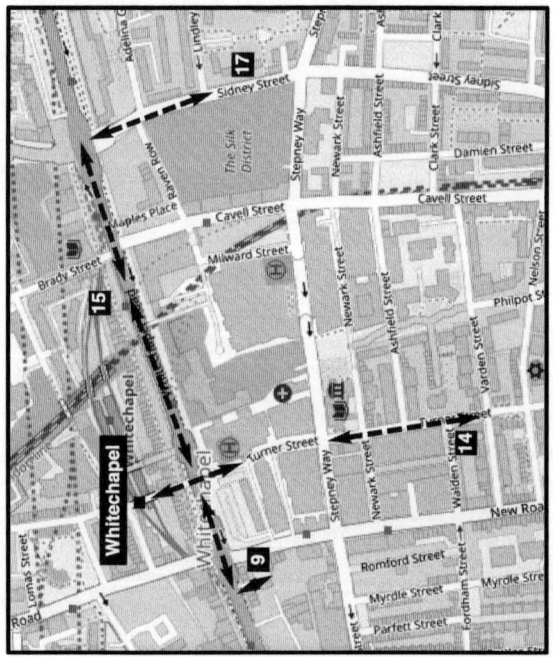

Map 6 – Whitechapel

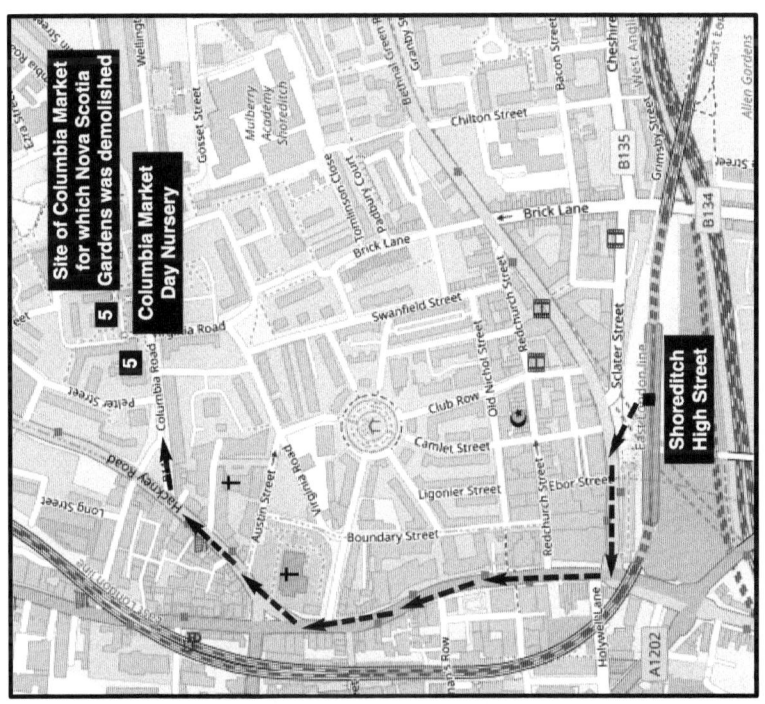

Map 7 – Shoreditch High Street

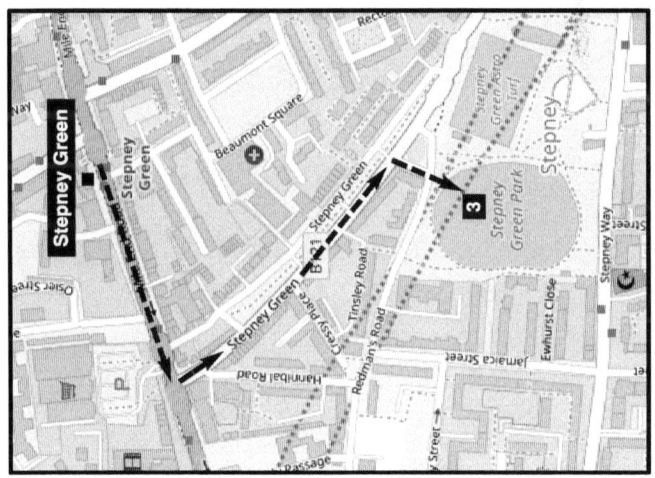

Map 8 – Stepney Green

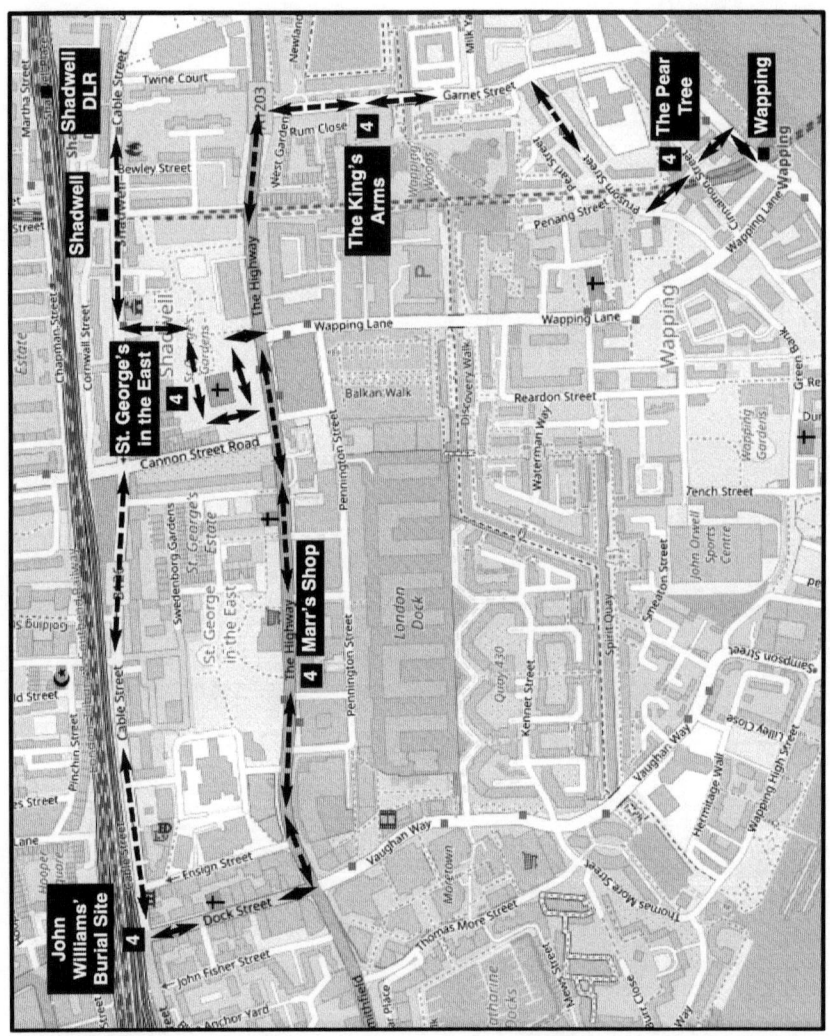

Map 9 – Shadwell & Wapping

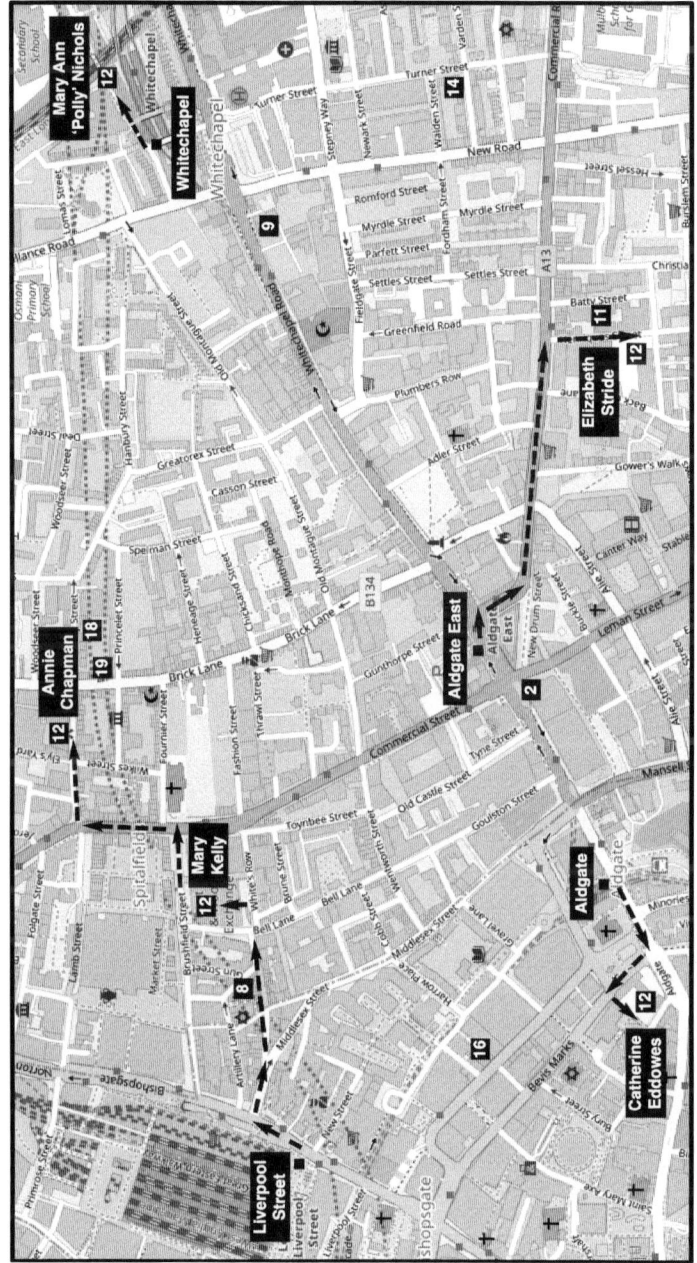

Map 10 – Jack the Ripper

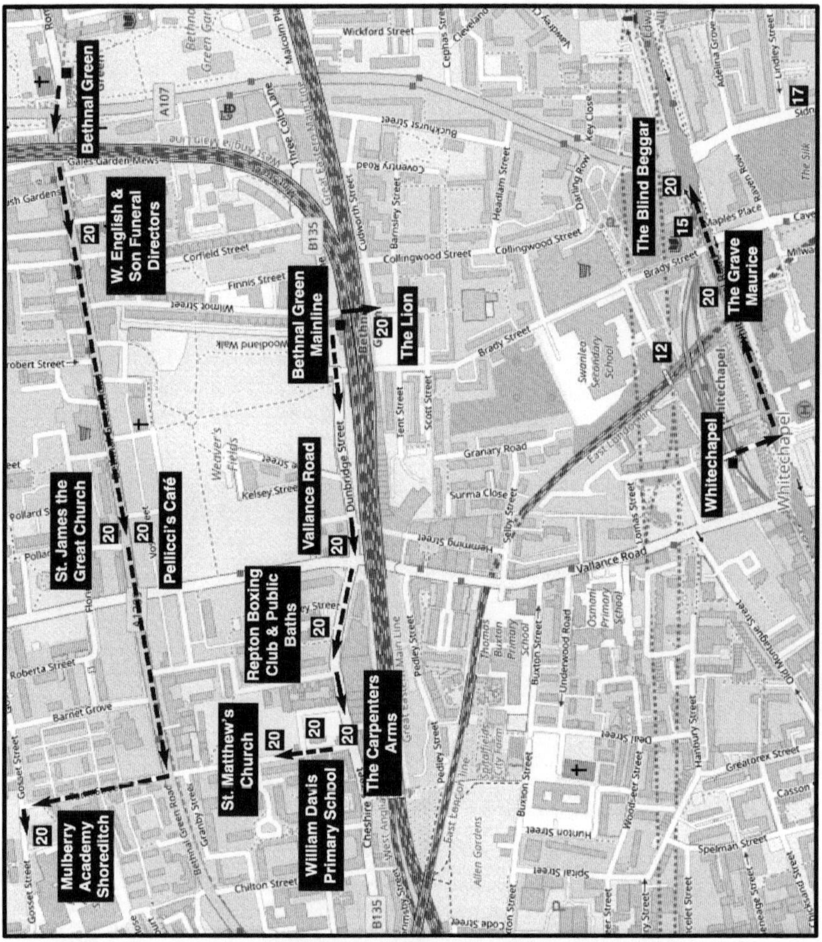

Map 11 – The Kray Twins

All maps generated with the help of OpenStreetMap
Location positions are defined from What3Words.com

THE KRAY TWINS WALK

Duration: 1¹/₂ - 2 hours
Start: Bethnal Green station   **Finish:** Whitechapel station

The tour uses the What3Words (3 words in bold with round brackets) application to identify locations as accurately as possible, and includes page references (bold numbers with round brackets) and photographic references (bold numbers with square brackets). Although London is a safe city, it should be noted that the tour is set in a non-tourist area of London with a higher than average crime rate – please take this into consideration when planning your visit. The tour starts at Bethnal Green Underground station (Central Line) and finishes at Whitechapel Underground station (Metropolitan, Circle, Overground and Elizabeth Lines). It follows a 'S' shape taking in a dozen places associated with the Kray twins, as well as other sites of general interest. The tour can be done in either direction, but if finishing at Whitechapel there is the added advantage of taking a drink in The Blind Beggar public house at the conclusion of the walk. The walk is over flat terrain.

❧ 1 ❧
BETHNAL GREEN - W. ENGLISH & SON FUNERAL DIRECTORS
⇐5 minutes ⇒

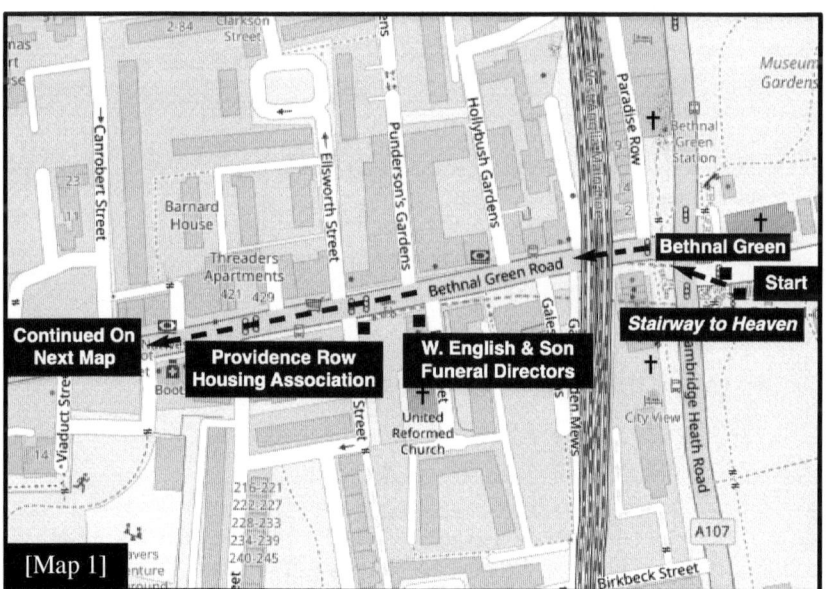

201

From Bethnal Green Underground station [**Map 1**] exit via the southeast exit and as you climb the stairs look to your right. You will see a piece of artwork entitled *Stairway to Heaven* (**chain.after.canny**) [**1**] by Harry Paticas. Unveiled in 2017, it commemorates the 173 people (62 of them children) who lost their lives on the night of the 3rd March 1943 as they tried to enter the railway station, which at the time was being used as an air raid shelter, when a woman carrying a baby stumbled over the 3rd step from the bottom causing others to fall on top of her. The entrance was dimly lit, and it had been raining earlier in the evening making the steps slippery. It was to be the biggest loss of civilian life in a single incident in the whole of World War II. The memorial comprises a stairway of 19 inverted steps overhanging a large concrete plinth. The names of the dead are included on the sides, and the staircase is perforated with 173 holes, one for each victim, so light can shine though. If you look behind you there is an earlier plaque [**2**] that also marks the tragedy.

Cross Cambridge Heath Road, or you may prefer to retrace your steps and take the southwest exit from the railway station, and proceed along Bethnal Green Road under the railway bridge. Stay on the left-hand side of the road, and on the corner of Pott Street (the 2nd turning) is W. English & Son Funeral Directors (**hurray.unable.potato**) (**178**).

❧ 2 ❧
W. ENGLISH & SON FUNERAL DIRECTORS - PELLICCI'S CAFÉ
⇐10 minutes ⇒

Continue walking along Bethnal Green Road. You will soon pass The Shakespeare public house at No. 460, and the adjacent Providence Row Housing Association offices (**learns.rice.loans**). The public house dates from 1842 and retains its original Victorian façade, while the first Providence Row Night Refuge was opened in 1860 at the back of Finsbury Square in a narrow street called

Providence Row. It only had 14 beds and was open to anybody regardless of race or religion. It later expanded and moved to a much larger building in Crispin Street, Spitalfields where by 1862 nearly 15,000 meals had been provided to the poor and destitute.

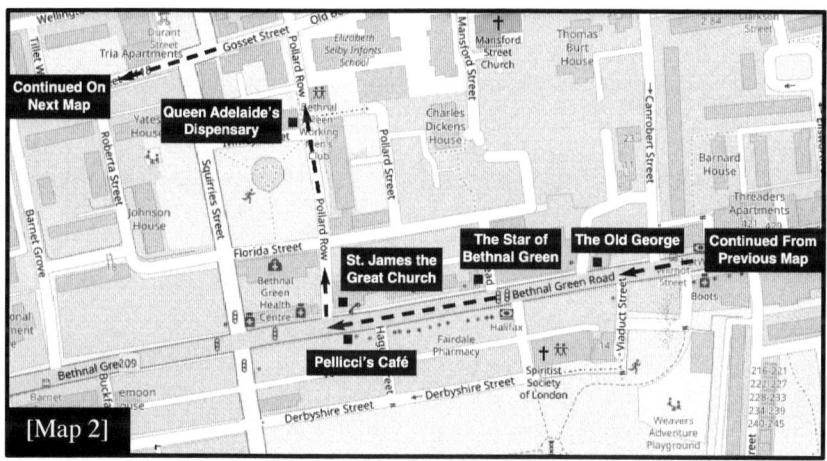

Two more original Victorian public houses you will pass are The Old George (**cliff.horns.ties**) and The Star of Bethnal Green (**prefer.mild.handy**) (both on your right) [**Map 2**]. Soon you will come across market stalls on your left, and at No. 332, also on your left, is Pellicci's Café (**things.spaces.trials**) (**180**).

❧ 3 ❧
PELLICCI'S CAFÉ - ST. JAMES THE GREAT CHURCH
⇐ 0 minutes ⇒

Immediately opposite Pellicci's Café is the former St. James the Great Church (**villa.bond.gossip**) (**183**) which is now a residential development.

❧ 4 ❧
ST. JAMES THE GREAT CHURCH- MULBERRY ACADEMY SHOREDITCH
⇐ 15 minutes ⇒

Cross over the road and go up Pollard Row beside the former St. James the Great Church. On your left you will pass Pollard Square, and at the corner with Ivimey Street you will see the former Queen Adelaide's Dispensary (**hardy.donor.dunes**) [**3**]. It is built in the Renaissance style, decorated with

203

carved fruits and flowers, and has a clock tower featuring the bust of Queen Adelaide. The funding was in part from a bequest of £100 left in Queen Adelaide's will for the setting up of a cholera dispensary at Warner Place in 1850. It was the Reverend Edward Coke (**184**) who raised £2,000 toward the building before you, which actually cost closer to £7,000 when finished. It was opened in 1866, just in time for another cholera outbreak which was to cost the lives 614 people from the local area. It continued as a hospital until 1961, then as a nurse's home until it was converted into flats in the 1990s.

[3]

Continue to the end of the road where you will turn left into Gosset Street [**Map 3**]. Walk a little past the 3rd turning on your left (Turin Street) where you will see the old and new buildings forming the Mulberry Academy Shoreditch (**back.gifted.half**) (**180**). Note the original name (Daniel Street School) in the brickwork. In fact, from here you are very close to Columbia Road (at the end of Gosset Street), the site of the murder of Carlo Ferrari (**37**).

❧ 5 ❧

MULBERRY ACADEMY SHOREDITCH - ST. MATTHEW'S CHURCH
⇐15 minutes ⇒

Retrace your steps and turn right into Turin Street. This road is made up of low-rise blocks of flats. On the left-hand side you will pass The Front Line building (**caged.scale.then**), a charity that focusses entirely on social work for children and families in Bethnal Green. Turin Street ends at Bethnal Green Road. Continue straight over into St. Matthew's Row. On your left-hand side is St. Matthew's Church (**trunk.homes.sushi**) (**184**).

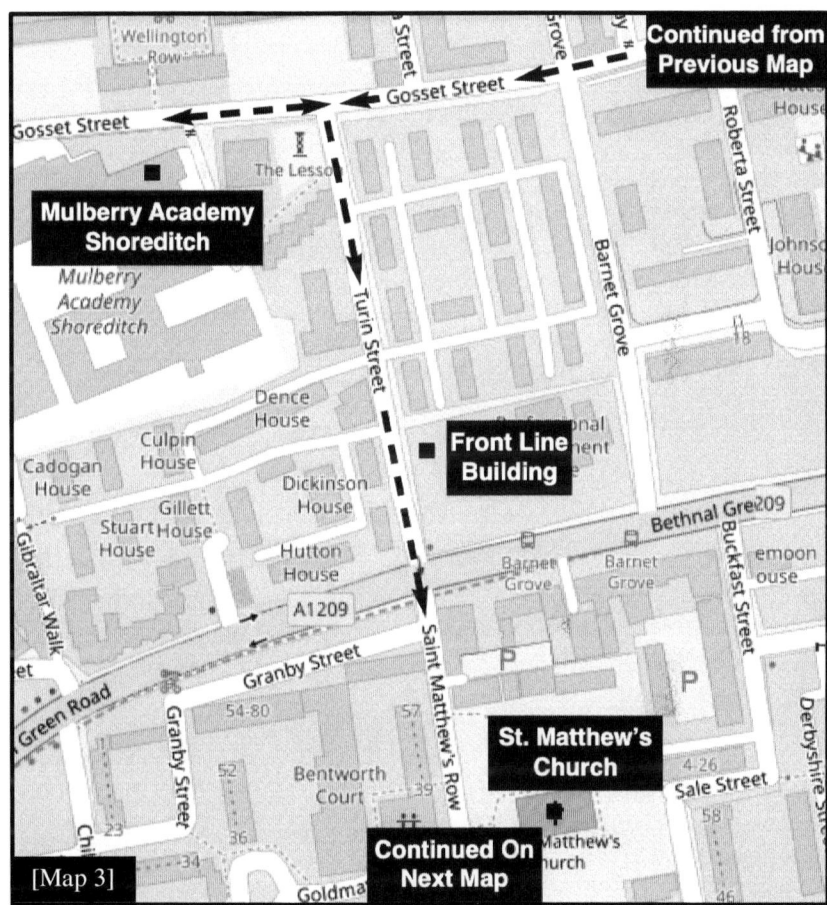

♨ 6 ♨
ST. MATTHEW'S CHURCH - WILLIAM DAVIS PRIMARY SCHOOL
⇐2 minutes ⇒

Continue along St. Matthew's Row [**Map 4**] to Wood Close on your left-hand side. The entrance to the William Davis Primary School (**piles.linen.ends**) (**187**) is in Wood Close. Note the similar brickwork to the Mulberry Academy Shoreditch, but without the inclusion of the school name.

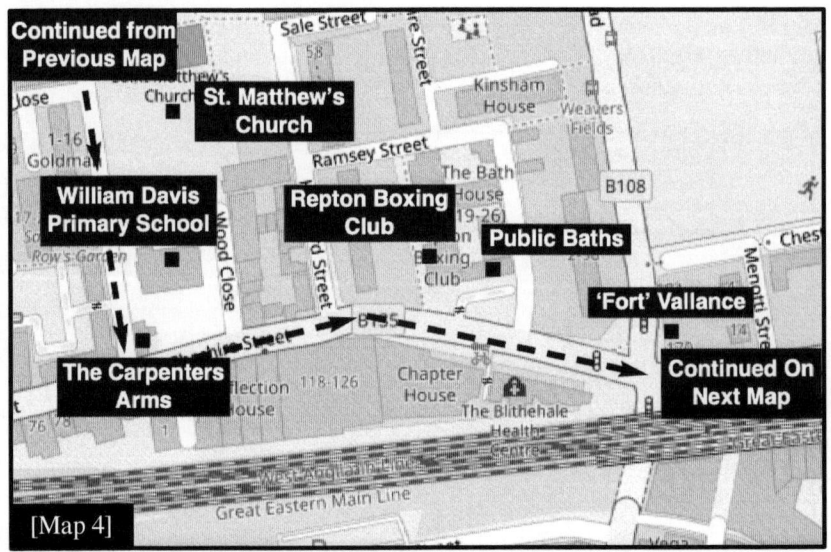

[Map 4]

❧ 7 ❧
WILLIAM DAVIS PRIMARY SCHOOL - THE CARPENTERS ARMS
⇦1 minute ⇨

At the end of St. Matthew's Row, and in the shadow of William Davis Primary School, is the Carpenters Arms public house (**guides.jolly.silk**) (**177**). You are now just over halfway on this tour so you might consider a break and refreshments at this establishment.

❧ 8 ❧
THE CARPENTERS ARMS - REPTON BOXING CLUB & PUBLIC BATHS
⇦5 minutes ⇨

At the junction of St. Matthew's Row and Cheshire Street (with the Carpenters Arms on your left) turn left and proceed east along Cheshire Street. Cheshire Street soon becomes Dunbridge Street. You will see the mainline railway viaduct running parallel to you on your right. Just past Hereford Street on your left-hand side you will see the Repton Boxing Club (**rotate.plays.boom**) (**181**) where the Kray twins learnt their legitimate trade. The entrance to the club is on your left but please note that it is not open to the public. Adjacent to the boxing club are the public baths.

❧ 9 ❧
REPTON BOXING CLUB & PUBLIC BATHS - VALLANCE ROAD
⇐2 minutes ⇒

Continue along Dunbridge Street to the next set of traffic lights. The location of where 'Fort Vallance' (**inform.shift.plays**) (**186**) once stood is on the north side close to the opposite corner (actually the 4th property from the corner) where you will see the plaque unveiled by Prince Charles on the 15th September 1988.

❧ 10 ❧
VALLANCE ROAD - THE LION
⇐10 minutes ⇒

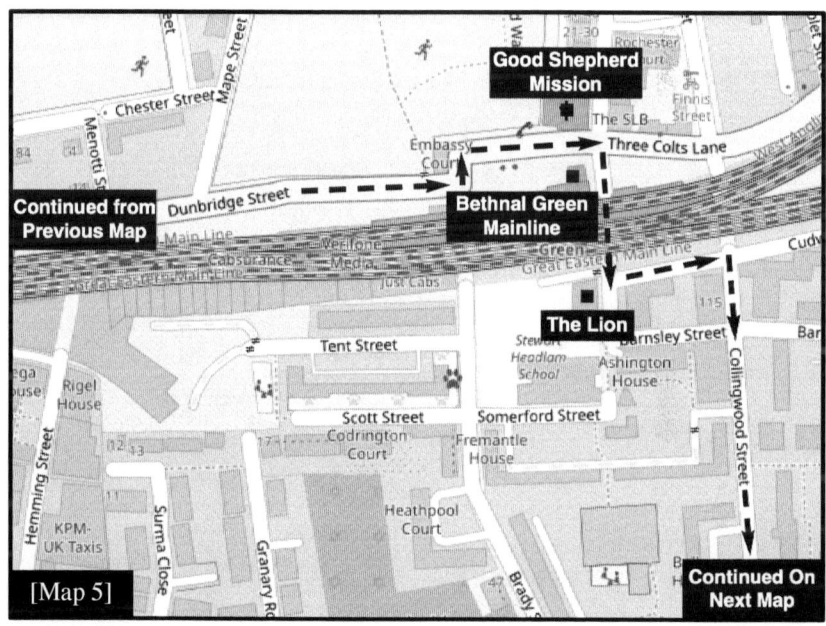

[Map 5]

Continue along Dunbridge Street [**Map 5**] keeping the railway viaduct to your right. You will note the multitude of businesses that have taken up residence in the railway arches, many of them relating to the servicing and repair of London black taxis cabs. At the end of Dunbridge Street there is a 'T' junction with Brady Street. Turn left and then right into Three Colts Lane.

On the left-hand side you will come to the Good Shepherd Mission (**leaps.filled.scans**), which occupies the site of the former Good Shepherd

Schools. Founded in 1856 it was, at first, a local Sunday School connected with St. Andrew's Church, which over the next decade became a day school situated in Mape Street. That building no longer exists since it was demolished to make way for The Great Eastern Railway, who provided funds for the current establishment in Three Colts Lane which opened in 1872. It was extended in 1934 and amalgamated with the King Edward Institution and George Yard Mission. Today, apart from church activities, the Mission runs a variety of early years activities, through to youth clubs, and adult programmes for vulnerable persons and those at risk of social exclusion. Opposite is the entrance to Bethnal Green mainline station. Turn right into Tapp Street and proceed under the railway bridge. The first building on your right as you immerge from passing under the railway line is The Lion public house (**belts.certified.woes**) (**179**) which today has been converted to residential flats.

❧ 11 ❧
THE LION - THE BLIND BEGGAR
⇐10 minutes ⇒

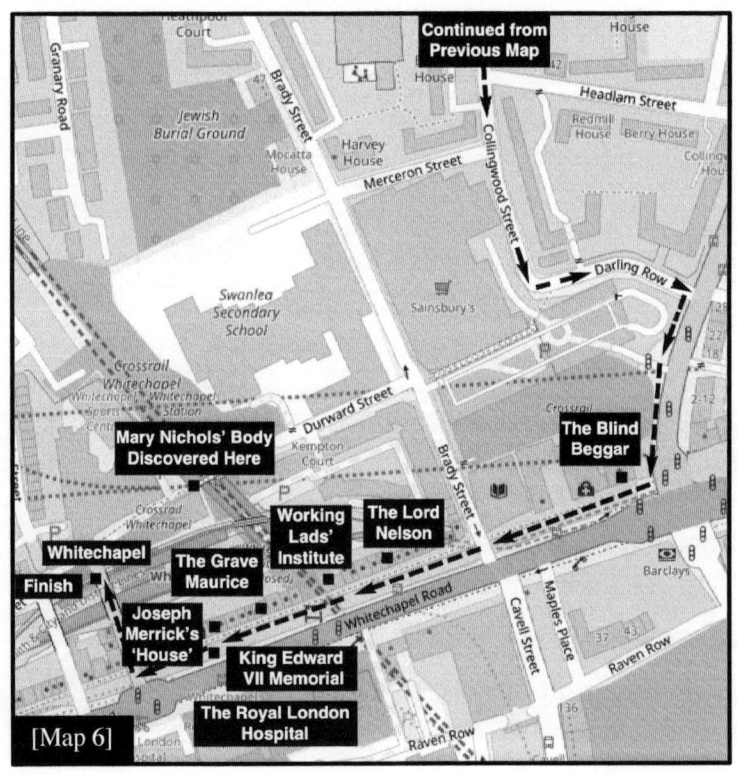

[Map 6]

Turn left into Cudworth Street, and then first right into Collingwood Street. Eventually Collingworth Street bears left and becomes Darling Row [**Map 6**]. Follow the road to the end at the 'T' junction with Cambridge Heath Road (where there is a Sainsbury's supermarket on the corner). Turn right and continue down Cambridge Heath Road to the next junction where there are traffic lights. At this major crossroads Mile End Road will be to your left, Whitechapel Road to your right, while if you go straight over you will be in Sidney Street and close to the where the Sidney Street Siege took place in 1911 (**petty.prom.cloth**) (**151**). However, you should turn right and immediately on your right you will see The Blind Beggar public house (**pushes.lists.notice**) (**176**). As you are nearly at the end of the tour you might wish to take refreshments at this infamous public house before continuing to the final location.

ᐉ 12 ᐉ
THE BLIND BEGGAR - THE GRAVE MAURICE
⇦2 minutes ⇨

[4]   [5]

From the Blind Beggar public house continue along Whitechapel Road which will soon become a street market. You will pass No. 299 on your left. This was the location of the Lord Nelson public house (**pump.thick.dared**) (**135**) where Martha Hardwick was murdered. Just a few shops further on, and next to the original entrance to Whitechapel station, you will see the Working Lads' Institute (**remedy.fines.simple**) [4] and [5]. This is where the inquest into the murder of Mary Nichols (**95**), the first of the canonical 5 Jack the Ripper murder victims, was held. When opened in 1885 its purpose was to keep young lads out of trouble and to provide academic classes. There was a fully equipped gym, a library, a large swimming pool, and even limited accommodation.

Just the other side of the railway station at No. 269 is the location of The Grave Maurice public house (**lands.wants.much**) (**178**). This is the last Kray twins location and from here to Whitechapel station simply continue walking along Whitechapel Road. Note the Victorian façade of the Royal London Hospital (**132**) on your left, and also the King Edward VII Memorial (**café.safe.person**) [6].

This drinking fountain is a reminder that the population of the area was mainly Jewish, for it was erected 'from subscriptions raised by Jewish inhabitants of the East End' and unveiled in 1912 by Charles Rothschild. The design includes bronze figures of the Angel of Peace [7], and the Angel of Justice with 2 cherubs – one has a needle and thread indicating the importance of the clothing industry to the area, and the other is reading a book signifying the importance of education [8]. On the opposite side is the Angel of Liberty also with 2 cherubs – one holds a ship to indicate that many locals were recently immigrants, while the second has a car illustrating progress away from the horse and cart [9].

Just by the memorial is No. 259 (**harder.exact.chains**) [10] at the back of which Joseph Merrick, better known as John Merrick 'The Elephant Man', could be viewed in a freak show. It was worked by his manager who would gather an audience outside the premises and explain that the Elephant Man was 'not here to frighten you but to enlighten you'. Once inside he would draw back a curtain to allow the gathered crowd a close up view of Merrick while telling them a brief outline of his life. The audience could also purchase as a pamphlet about Merrick.

Continue to Court Street, on your right, which will take you to the entrance of Whitechapel station on the Metropolitan, District, Overground and Elizabeth Lines. Congratulations you have now completed the tour, but if you wish to make a slight detour the road at the end of Court Street is Durward Street where if you turn right you will find the spot (**jolly.orange.monks**) where the body Mary Nichols (**95**) was discovered. The location is just beyond Trinity Hall [11] next to the Durward Street exit from Whitechapel station.

ACKNOWLEDGMENTS

All the photographs in this publication, excepted where acknowledged, are by the author, or already in the public domain (www.commons.wikimedia.org). Particularly useful sources of illustrations include the Associated Newspapers Limited archive, and original publications such as *The Illustrated Police News*, *The Penny Illustrated Paper*, *Funny Folks Magazine*, *London Old & New*, and *Living London* as well as old postcards. The illustrations for pages 39, 40, 42, 43, 47, and 204 are courtesy of the Wellcome Library, London. The maps on pages 50 and 60 were created using www.theundegroundmap.com, while all other maps used www.openstreetmap.org, with physical locations being defined by www.What3Words.com.

REFERENCES & FURTHER READING

JACK THE RIPPER

Begg, Paul, *Jack the Ripper The Definitive History*, 310 pages, Pearson Education Limited, (2003), ISBN: 978-0-582506-31-2.

Clack, Robert & Hutchinson, Philip, *The London of Jack the Ripper Then and Now*, 190 pages, Breedon Books Publishing, (2007), ISBN: 978-1-859836-00-2.

Evans, Stuart P. & Rumbelow, Donald, *Jack the Ripper Scotland Yard Investigates*, 303 pages, Sutton Publishing, (2006), ISBN: 978-0-750942-28-7.

Evans, Stuart P. & Skinner, Keith, *The Ultimate Jack the Ripper Companion*, 758 pages, Carroll & Graf, (2000), ISBN: 978-0-786709-26-7.

Evans, Stuart P. & Skinner, Keith, *Jack the Ripper and the Whitechapel Murders*, 12 pages, Public Record Office, (2002), ISBN: 978-1-903365-39-7.

Fido, Martin, *The Crimes, Detection & Death of Jack the Ripper*, 241 pages, Weidenfeld & Nicolson, ISBN: 978-0-297791-36-2.

Horsler, Val, *Jack the Ripper*, 112 pages, The National Archives, (2007), ISBN: 978-1-905615-14-8.

Sugden, Philip, *The Complete History of Jack the Ripper*, 532 pages, Carroll & Graf, (1994), ISBN: 978-0-786709-32-8.

www.casebook.org – an excellent source of information on Jack the Ripper which also has links to the contemporary records.

www.jack-the-ripper.org – another excellent source of information on everything Jack the Ripper.

www.whitechapelsociety.com – website of The Whitechapel Society, a long-established historical society dedicated to studies of Jack the Ripper as well as wider aspects of Victorian and Edwardian east London.

OTHER MURDERS

Barker, Felix & Silvester-Carr, Denise, *The Black Plaque Guide to London*, 344 pages, Constable and Company Ltd, (1987), ISBN: 978-0-094665-10-1.

Bondeson, Jan, *Victorian Murders*, 320 pages, Amberley Publishing, (2017), ISBN: 978-1-445666-30-3.

Herber, Mark, *Criminal London*, 207 pages, Phillimore & Co. Ltd., (2002), ISBN: 978-1-860771-99-6.

Lane, Brian, *The Murder Guide to London*, 104 pages, Magpie, (1992), ISBN: 978-1-858130-64-4.

Jones, Steve, *London ... The Sinister Side*, 87 pages, Wicked Publications, (1992), ISBN: 978-1-870000-00-0.

Moss, Alan & Skinner, Keith, *Scotland Yard's History of Crime in 100 Objects*, 400 pages, The History Press, (2015), ISBN: 978-0-750962-87-2.

Sellwood, Arthur & Sellwood, Mary, *Death Ride from Fenchurch Street and other Victorian Railway Murders*, 157 pages, Amberley Publishing Plc, (2009), ISBN: 978-1-848684-95-9.

Wilson, Colin & Wilson, Damon, *World Famous Gaslight Murder*, 119 pages, Magpie Books Ltd, (1992), ISBN: 978-1-854871-53-4.

LONDON

Sims, George R., *Living London*, Volumes I-III, Cassell and Company, Limited, (1903).

Weinreb, Ben (Editor) & Hibbert, Christopher (Editor), *The London Encyclopaedia*, 1120 pages, MacMillan Reference, (2010), ISBN: 978-1-405049-25-2.

Walford, Edward, *Old and New London: A narrative of its History, its People, and its Places*, Volumes I-VI, Cassell & Company, Limited, (1902).

If you enjoyed this publication you may also like ...

Available in all good bookshops or direct from the
publisher at www.crime4u.com

If you enjoyed this publication you may also like …

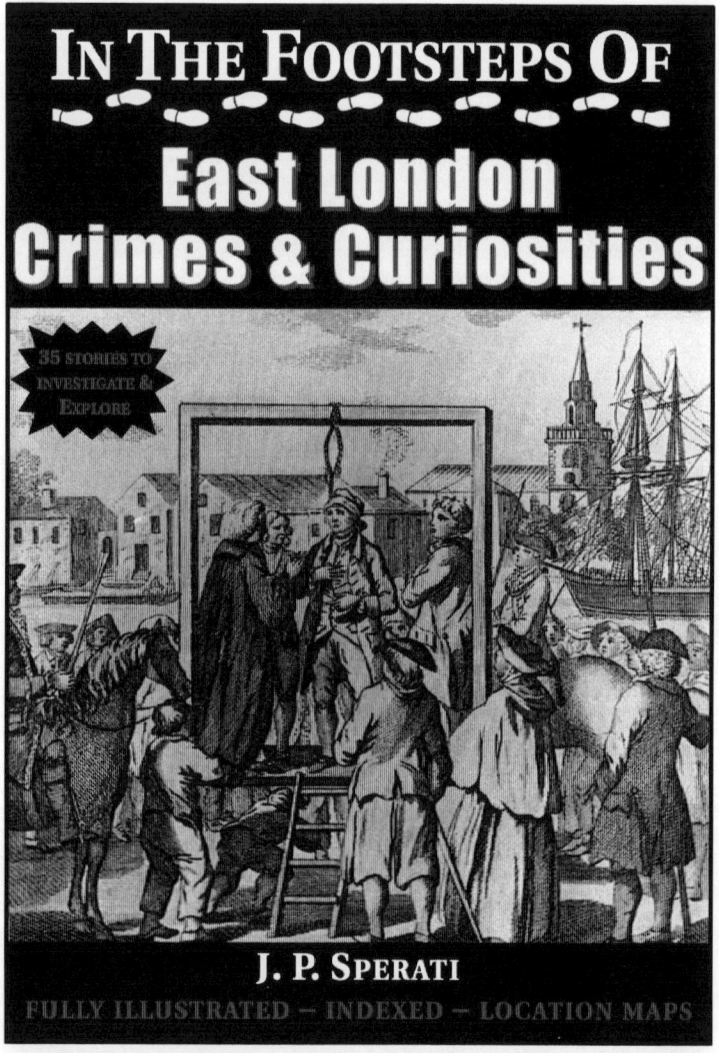